Penguin Modern Poets

VOLUME 11

Michael Donaghy was born in the Bronx, New York, in 1954 and studied at Fordham University and the University of Chicago, where he was poetry editor of the *Chicago Review*. He moved to Britain in 1985 and lives in north London. His collections to date are *Shibboleth* (1988), which won the Whitbread Prize for Poetry and the Geoffrey Faber Memorial Prize, and *Errata* (1993), for which he received an Arts Council Writers Award and a grant from the Ingram Merrill Foundation.

Andrew Motion was born in 1952 and educated at University College, Oxford. He was editor of *Poetry Review*, and among his poetry collections are *Dangerous Play* (1985), *Love in a Life* (1991), *The Price of Everything* (1994) and *Salt Water* (1997). He has also written critical studies; biographies, notably his acclaimed *Philip Larkin: A Writer's Life* (1993); and two novels. He has edited William Barnes's *Selected Poems* (Penguin Classics) and, with Blake Morrison, *The Penguin Book of Contemporary British Poetry*. His work has won many prizes, including the John Llewellyn Rhys Memorial Prize, the Somerset Maugham Award and the Whitbread Prize for Biography. He is Professor of Creative Writing at the University of East Anglia.

Hugo Williams was born in Windsor in 1942, the son of actor and playwright Hugh Williams. His first poems were published while he was still at school, after which he worked on the *London Magazine* for ten years. Since then he has earned his living from journalism and teaching. He was poetry editor and television critic of the *New Statesman*, theatre critic of the *Sunday Correspondent*, and he is now film critic of *Harper's & Queen*. He writes the 'Freelance' column for *The Times Literary Supplement* and pop music pieces for *Punch*. As well as eight books of poems, he has published two travel books, *All the Time in the World* and *No Particular Place to Go*, and a book of columns, *Freelancing*.

The Penguin Modern Poets Series

Penguin Modern Poets

VOLUME 11

MICHAEL DONAGHY
ANDREW MOTION
HUGO WILLIAMS

PENGUIN BOOKS

Published by the Penguin Group
Penguin Books Ltd, 27 Wrights Lane, London W8 5TZ, England
Penguin Books USA Inc., 375 Hudson Street, New York, New York 10014, USA
Penguin Books Australia Ltd, Ringwood, Victoria, Australia
Penguin Books Canada Ltd, 10 Alcorn Avenue, Toronto, Ontario, Canada M4V 3B2
Penguin Books (NZ) Ltd, 182 – 190 Wairau Road, Auckland 10, New Zealand

Penguin Books Ltd, Registered Offices: Harmondsworth, Middlesex, England

This selection first published 1997
10 9 8 7 6 5 4 3 2 1

Set in 10.5/13pt Monotype Garamond
Typeset by Rowland Phototypesetting Ltd, Bury St Edmunds, Suffolk
Printed in England by Clays Ltd, St Ives plc

Contents

Michael Donaghy

City of God

When he failed the seminary he came back home
to the Bronx and sat in a back pew
of St Mary's every night reciting the Mass
from memory – quietly, continually –
into his deranged overcoat.
He knew the local phone book off by heart.
He had a system, he'd explain,
perfected by Dominicans in the Renaissance.

To every notion they assigned a saint
to every saint an altar in a transept of the church.
Glancing up, column by column, altar by altar,
they could remember any prayer they chose.
He'd used it for exams, but the room went wrong –
a strip-lit box exploding slowly as he fainted.
They found his closet papered floor to ceiling
with razored passages from St Augustine.

He needed a perfect cathedral in his head,
he'd whisper, so that by careful scrutiny
the mind inside the cathedral inside the mind
could find the secret order of the world
and remember every drop on every face
in every summer thunderstorm.
And that, he'd insist, looking beyond you,
is why he came home.

I walked him back one evening as the snow
hushed the precincts of his vast invisible temple.
Here was Bruno Street where Bernadette
collapsed, bleeding through her skirt
and died, he had heard, in a state of mortal sin;

here, the site of the bakery fire where Peter stood
screaming on the red-hot fire escape,
his bare feet blistering before he jumped;
and here the storefront voodoo church beneath the 'el'
where the Cuban *bruja* bought black candles,
its window strange with plaster saints and seashells.

The brother

Dropping a canapé in my beaujolais
At some reception, opening or launch,
I recall, briefly, the brother I never had
Presiding at less worldly rituals:
The only man at my wedding not wearing a tie;
Avuncular, swaddling my nephew over the font;
Thumbing cool oil on our mother's forehead
In the darkened room, the bells and frankincense . . .
While the prodigal sweats in the strip-lit corridor.

Now, picture us facing each other, myself and the brother
I never met: two profiles in silhouette,
Or else a chalice, depending how you look.
Imagine that's this polystyrene cup.
I must break bread with my own flesh and blood.

Caliban's books

Hair oil, boiled sweets, chalk dust, squid's ink . . .
Bear with me. I'm trying to conjure my father,
age fourteen, as Caliban – picked by Mr Quinn
for the role he was born to play because
'I was the handsomest boy at school'
he'll say, straight faced, at fifty.
This isn't easy. I've only half the spell,
and I won't be born for twenty years.
I'm trying for rainlight on Belfast Lough
and listening for a small, blunt accent
barking over the hiss of a stove getting louder like surf.
But how can I read when the schoolroom's gone
black as the hold of a ship? Start again.

Hair oil, boiled sweets . . .
But his paperbacks are crumbling in my hands,
seachanged bouquets, each brown page
scribbled on, underlined, memorized,
forgotten like used pornography:
The Pocket Treasury of English Verse
How to Win Friends and Influence People
Thirty Days to a More Powerful Vocabulary.

Fish stink, pitch stink, seaspray, cedarwood . . .
I seem to have brought us to the port of Naples,
midnight, to a shadow below deck
dreaming of a distant island.
So many years, so many ports ago!
The moment comes. It slips from the hold
and knucklewalks across the dark piazza
sobbing *maestro! maestro!* But the duke's long dead
and all his magic books are drowned.

Held

Not in the sense that this snapshot, a girl in a garden,
Is named for its subject, or saves her from ageing,
Not as this ammonite changed like a sinner to minerals
Heavy and cold on my palm is immortal,
But as we stopped for the sound of the lakefront one
    morning
Before the dawn chorus of sprinklers and starlings.

Not as this hieroglyph chiselled by Hittites in lazuli,
Spiral and faint, is a word for 'unending',
Nor as the hands, crown and heart in the emblem of
    Claddagh,
Pewter and plain on that ring mean for ever,
But as we stood at the window together, in silence,
Precisely twelve minutes by candlelight waiting for thunder.

THE HUNTER'S PURSE

      is the last unshattered 78
by 'Patrolman Jack O'Ryan, violin',
a Sligo fiddler in dry America.

A legend, he played Manhattan's ceilidhs,
fell asleep drunk one snowy Christmas
on a Central Park bench and froze solid.
They shipped his corpse home, like his records.

This record's record is its lunar surface.
I wouldn't risk my stylus to this gouge,
or this crater left by a flick of ash –

When Anne Quinn got hold of it back in Kilrush,
she took her fiddle to her shoulder
and cranked the new Horn of Plenty
Victrola over and over and over,
and scratched along until she had it right
or until her father shouted

    'We'll have *no* more
    Of *that* tune
    In *this* house to*night*.'

She slipped out back and strapped the contraption
to the parcel rack and rode her bike
to a far field, by moonlight.

It skips. The penny I used for ballast slips.
O'Ryan's fiddle pops, and hiccoughs
back to this, back to this, back to this:
a napping snowman with a fiddlecase;

a flask of bootleg under his belt;
three stars; a gramophone on a pushbike;
a cigarette's glow from a far field;
over and over, three bars in common time.

A REPRIEVE

Realizing that few of the many tunes remembered from boyhood days
... were known to the galaxy of Irish musicians domiciled in Chicago,
the writer decided to have them preserved in musical notation. This was
the initial step in a congenial work which has filled in the interludes of a
busy and eventful life.

Police Chief Francis O'Neill
Irish Folk Music: A Fascinating Hobby, With Some Account of Related Subjects
(Chicago, 1910)

Here in Chicago it's almost dawn
and quiet in the cell in Deering Street stationhouse
apart from the first birds at the window and the milkwagon
and the soft slap of the club in Chief O'Neill's palm.
'Think it over,' he says, 'but don't take all day.'
Nolan's hands are brown with a Chinaman's blood.
But if he agrees to play three jigs
slowly, so O'Neill can take them down,
he can walk home, change clothes,
and disappear past the stockyards and across the tracks.

Indiana is waiting. O'Neill lowers his eyes,
knowing the Chinaman's face will heal, the Great Lakes
roll in their cold grey sheets and wake,
picket lines will be charged, girls raped
in the sweatshops, the clapboard tenements burn.
And he knows that Nolan will be gone by then,
the coppery stains wiped from the keys of the blackwood
    flute.

Five thousand miles away Connaught sleeps.
The coast lights dwindle out along the west.
But there's music here in this lamplit cell,
and O'Neill scratching in his manuscript like a monk
at his illuminations, and Nolan's sweet tone breaking
as he tries to phrase a jig the same way twice:
'The Limerick Rake' or 'Tell her I am' or 'My Darling
    Asleep'.

A REPERTOIRE

'*Play us one we've never heard before*'
we'd ask this old guy in our neighbourhood.
He'd rosin up a good three or four
seconds, stalling, but he always could.
This was the Bronx in 1971,
when every night the sky was pink with arson.
He ran a bar beneath the 'el', the Blarney Stone,
and there one Easter day he sat us down
and made us tape as much as he could play;
I gave you these. Make sure you put that down
meaning all he didn't have to say.

All that summer we slept on fire escapes,
or tried to sleep, while sirens or the brass
from our neighbour's Tito Puente tapes
kept us up and made us late for Mass.
I found our back door bent back to admit
beneath the thick sweet reek of grass
a nest of needles, bottlecaps and shit.
By August Tom had sold the Blarney Stone
to Puerto Ricans, paid his debts in cash
but left enough to fly his body home.

The bar still rises from the South Bronx ash,
its yellow neon buzzing in the noonday
dark beneath the el, a sheet-steel door
bolted where he played each second Sunday.
Play me one I've never heard before
I'd say, and whether he recalled those notes,
or made them up, or – since it was Tom who played –
whether it was 'something in his blood'
(cancer, and he was childless and afraid)
I couldn't tell you. And he always would.

DOWN

The stars are shuffling slowly round
Burning in the dark
Upon the lips of angry men
Drinking in the park.
Five thousand fed. I read it in
The Gospel of St Mark.

Helicopters insect round
Above the burnt-out cars.
Here where Gospel testified
Between the wars
His harp of darkness cried and prayed
To bottleneck guitars.

Tell me why's you cryin' baby?
I sure would like to know.
Tell me why's you cryin' baby
I sure would like to know . . .
Some words I can't make out, and then,
  . . . I'll come walkin' through that door.

These flattened thirds and sevenths
Justified the Blues:
Intervals ruled by celestial laws,
Horse, and booze.
Woke up this morning's just the kind
Of line he couldn't use.

Cicadas carve across this night
Their lapidary phrase,
And the darkness children fear
They continually praise.
The darkness children fear, they
Continually praise.

THEODORA, THEODORA

Tomorrow, Parnassus. Tonight, outside the taverna,
you wait in the darkened coach alone
flaking *kif* into a roll-up by the dashboard light.
Plates crash. The band risk a verse or two
of a song they played before the war in brothels
where you fucked, gambled and somehow failed
to die; a song about a girl who didn't.
For love. Slum music. Knives and despair.
Softly you sing what words you can remember.

There are stars in the verse, and two brothers,
hashish, wisteria, a straight razor. You can't recall
the name of the song or the name of the girl
who bleeds to death at dawn by birdsong before the basilica,
but they're the same. It's been so long.
The bishops banned it, and the generals,
and somehow even you – how else could you forget –
because these songs have backstreets much like this,
bile and retsina. Streets the cops don't like.

Sixteen bars then into Zorba. The tour-group clap,
snap pictures, then stumble on board laughing
in accents of Buenos Aires or Chicago,
where coach drivers wait outside bars on the south side,
singing softly, for no one but themselves tonight,
of girls who bleed for love. *'Theodora'*.
You remember. *'Theodora'*. Singing too loud,
you take the slow road back to the hotel.

THE NATURAL AND SOCIAL SCIENCES

We come to Straidkilly to watch the tide go out.
A man is loading a wicker basket
With small, complicated pink crabs.
'Have we missed it?' we ask, 'the tide?'
And he, with sincere assurance,
'It'll be back.'

A girl inspects an upside-down bike
On the road to Tubbercurry.
I stop to help but she rights it on its wheels,
Shoves off, ticking, in the light rain.

Musicians in the kitchen, Sunday morning in Gweedore.
An American with a tape recorder and a yellow notebook.
'What was the name of that last one?'
The piper shrugs and points to the dark corner.
'Ask my father.'
The American writes 'Ask My Father.'

THE CLASSICS

I remember it like it was last night.
Chicago, the back room of Flanagan's
malignant with accordions and cigarettes,

Joe Cooley bent above his Paolo Soprani,
its asthmatic bellows pumping as if to revive
the half corpse strapped about it.
It's five a.m. Everyone's packed up.
His brother Seamus grabs Joe's elbow mid-arpeggio,
Wake up man. We have to catch a train.
His eyelids fluttering, opening. The astonishment . . .

I saw this happen. Or heard it told so well
I've staged the whole drunk memory.
What does it matter now? It's ancient history.
Who can name them? Where lie their bones and armour?

Our life stories

What did they call that ball in Citizen Kane?
That crystal blizzardball forecasting his past?
Surely I know the name. Your mum's souvenir
of Blackpool, underwater, in winter –
say we dropped it. What would we say we broke?
And see what it says when you turn it over . . .

I dreamt the little Christmas dome I owned
slipped my soapy fingers and exploded.
Baby Jesus and the Virgin Mother
twitching on the lino like dying guppies.
Let's shake this up and change the weather.

Catch! This marvellous drop, like its own tear,
has leaked for years. The tiny ferris wheel has surfaced
in an oval bubble where it never snows
and little by little all is forgotten. Shhh!
Let's hold the sad toy storms in which we're held,
let's hold them gingerly above the bed,
bubbles gulping contentedly, as we rock them to sleep,
flurries aswim by our gentle skill,
their names on the tips of our tongues.

Liverpool

Ever been tattooed? It takes a whim of iron,
takes sweating in the antiseptic-stinking parlour,
nothing to read but motorcycle magazines
before the blood-sopped cotton and, of course, the needle,
all for – at best – some Chinese dragon.
But mostly they do hearts,

hearts skewered, blurry, spurting like the Sacred Heart
on the arms of bikers and sailors.
Even in prison they get by with biro ink and broken glass,
carving hearts into their arms and shoulders.
But women's are more intimate. They hide theirs,
under shirts and jeans, in order to bestow them.

Like Tracy, who confessed she'd had hers done
one legless weekend with her ex.
Heart. Arrow. Even the bastard's initials, R. J. L.,
somewhere where it hurt, she said,
and when I asked her where, snapped 'Liverpool!'

Wherever it was, she'd had it sliced away
leaving a scar, she said, pink and glassy,
but small, and better than having his mark on her,

(that self same mark of Valentinus,
who was flayed for love, but who never
– so the cardinals now say – existed.
Desanctified, apocryphal, like Christopher,
like the scar you never showed me, Trace,
your (   ), your ex, your 'Liverpool'.)

Still, when I unwrap the odd anonymous note
I let myself believe that it's from you.

Machines

Dearest, note how these two are alike:
This harpsichord pavane by Purcell
And the racer's twelve-speed bike.

The machinery of grace is always simple.
This chrome trapezoid, one wheel connected
To another of concentric gears,
Which Ptolemy dreamt of and Schwinn perfected,
Is gone. The cyclist, not the cycle, steers.
And in the playing, Purcell's chords are played away.

So this talk, or touch if I were there,
Should work its effortless gadgetry of love,
Like Dante's heaven, and melt into the air.

If it doesn't, of course, I've fallen. So much is chance,
So much agility, desire and feverish care,
As bicyclists and harpsichordists prove

Who only by moving can balance,
Only by balancing move.

Pentecost

The neighbours hammered on the walls all night,
Outraged by the noise we made in bed.
Still, we kept it up until by first light
We'd said everything that could be said.

Undaunted, we began to mewl and roar
As if desire had stripped itself of words.
Remember when we made those sounds before?
When we built a tower heavenwards
They were our reward for blasphemy.
And then again, two thousand years ago,
We huddled in a room in Galilee
Speaking languages we didn't know,
While amethyst uraeuses of flame
Hissed above us. We recalled the tower
And the tongues. We knew this was the same.
But love had turned the curse into a power.

See? It's something that we've always known:
Though we command the language of desire,
The voice of ecstasy is not our own.
We long to lose ourselves amid the choir
Of the salmon twilight and the mackerel sky,
The very air we take into our lungs,
And the rhododendron's cry.

And when you lick the sweat along my thigh,
Dearest, we renew the gift of tongues.

Cruising Byzantium

The saved, say firemen, sometimes return,
Enduring the inferno of the flat
To fetch the family photos. And they burn
Not for cash, cashmere coat nor cat,
Nor, as they momently suppose, for love.
They perish for the heraldries of light
And not such lives as these are emblem of.
But the saved, say firemen, are sometimes right.

Have you seen our holiday snaps from Greece?
Each Virgin burns in incandescent wonder
From her gold mosaic altarpiece.
This one was smashed by Gothic boot boys under
Orders from an Emperor who burned
The icon painters for idolatry.
Before her ruined face the faithful learned
The comet's path to a celestial sea.
And look. Here's you in skintight scuba gear
Winking through the window of your mask!
You have become the fetish that you wear.
I know precisely what you're going to ask;
Though golden in the Adriatic haze
You've waded to your thighs in molten light,
Your second skin aglitter in the sprays,
Your first it was we brought to bed that night.
And yet I'd almost brave the flames to keep
This idyll of perversity from burning.

Each photo frames a door beyond which, deep
Within the Patriarchate of my yearning,
The marble pavements surge with evensong.
But firemen say the saved are sometimes wrong.

The present

For the present there is just one moon,
though every level pond gives back another.

But the bright disc shining in the black lagoon,
perceived by astrophysicist and lover,

is milliseconds old. And even that light's
seven minutes older than its source.

And the stars we think we see on moonless nights
are long extinguished. And, of course,

this very moment, as you read this line,
is literally gone before you know it.

Forget the here-and-now. We have no time
but this device of wantonness and wit.

Make me this present then: your hand in mine,
and we'll live out our lives in it.

Analysand

Judges 12: 5–6

I've had an important dream. But that can wait.
I want to talk about Ephraim Herrero
And the cobalt-blue tattoo of Mexico
That graced his arm above the wrist.

We were his disciples back in school.
The hours I spent echoing his accent,
Facing off to the mirror, smoothing my jacket
Over the bulge of a kitchen knife . . .

Once he held a razor to my throat . . .
But we've been over that a hundred times.
Did I tell you he won the Latin prize?
So you see it was more than contempt and fear

That drew us to him. The day that he got done
For selling envelopes of snow in May
Behind Our Lady of Guadalupe
We were as much relieved as lost.

When the day of judgement came we were in court
Backing the loser, the soul of perjury
Wearing a tie he must have stolen from me
And someone else's Sunday suit.

It was a kick to see him so afraid.
And when he took the stand and raised his hand,
And his sleeve went south of the Rio Grande
I saw at once which side I was on.

Which brings me to the dream, if we have time.
I'm wading across a freezing river at night
Dressed in that suit and tie. A searchlight
Catches me mid-stream. I try to speak.

but someone steps between me and the beam.
The stars come out as if for an eclipse.
Slowly he raises his finger to his lips.
I wake before he makes that tearing sound.

Remembering steps to dances learned last night

Massive my heart, the heart of a hero, I knew it,
Though I was ten, pimpled, squint eyed, dung spattered.
I strung a bow, and memorized a brief heroic song
(I'll sing it for you later), left my goats in my father's yard,
And then went down to the ship.
Many men massed at the dock, loud their laughter.
But the king listened, noted my name, gave me wine,
A little patriotic speech, and sent me home
To the goats and the tedium and the ruminant years.
Once I made a song about the king and his distant
        plundering
And the hoard of memories, wondrous, he was gathering.
It's a shame you didn't bring your guitar.

Then one summer, when I was older,
And the king was long since missing in action,
Men came from Achaea to court the lonely queen.
The nights got loud with drums and laughter echoing from
        the palace,
Women's laughter, and the smell of roasted lamb.
What would you have done? I pounded on the gates one
        morning,
Rattled my arrows and stamped and sang about my
        hero-heart.
They seemed to understand . . . Or didn't mind my lying,
And they opened the gates on another world.
Beauty. Deception. Of weaving, of magic and of the edge of
        the known world
When the light fails, and you fall dead drunk across the table,
All these we learnt in our feasts and games amid the
        grey-eyed women.

Clever men and many we waited, the queen to choose
  among.
I know you came to hear me sing about the night the king
  came home,
When hero slaughtered hero in the rushlit hall,
Blood speckling the white clay walls wine-dark.
I can't. I'd stepped outside when the music stopped
  mid-tune.
Alone in the dark grove, I heard no sound but distant
  insects,
And the sound of water, mine, against the palace wall.
And then I heard their screams, the men and women I'd
  spent that summer with.

What would you have done?
I staggered home in the dawn rain, still half drunk,
Forgetting one by one the names of my dead friends,
Remembering steps to dances learnt that night, that very
  night,
Back to my goats, goat stink, goat cheese, the governing of
  goats.

'Smith'

What is this fear before the unctuous teller?
Why does it seem to take a forger's nerve
To make my signature come naturally?
Naturally? But every signature's
A trick we learn to do, consistently,
Like Queequeg's cross, or Whistler's butterfly.
Perhaps some childhood spectre clamps my hand
Every time I'm asked to sign my name.

Maybe it's Sister Bridget Agatha
Who drilled her class in Christ and penmanship
And sneered 'affected' at my seven-year-old scrawl.
True, it was unreadably ornate
And only one of five that I'd developed,
But try as I might I couldn't recall
The signature that I'd been born with.

Later, in my teens, I brought a girl,
My first, to see the Rodin exhibition.
I must have ranted on before each bronze;
'Metal of blood and honey . . .' Pure Sir Kenneth Clark.
And those were indeed the feelings I wanted to have,
But I could tell that she was unimpressed.
She fetched our coats. I signed the visitors' book,
My name embarrassed back into mere words.

No, I'm sure it all began years later.
I was twenty, and the girl was even younger.
We chose the hottest August night on record
And a hotel with no air-conditioning.
We tried to look adult. She wore her heels
And leant against the cigarette machine as,

Arching an eyebrow, I added to the register
The name I'd practised into spontaneity –
Surely it wasn't – *Mr and Mrs Smith?*
It's all so long ago and lost to me,
And yet I remember a moment so pure,
In every infinite detail indelible,
When I cupped her hips between my hands,
Balancing her in her slippery ride
And looked up to her eyes . . .

Dear friend, whatever is most true in me
Lives now and for ever in that instant,
The night I forged a hand, not mine, not anyone's,
And in that tiny furnace of a room,
Forged a thing unalterable as iron.

Letter

It's stopped this morning, nine hours deep
And blank in the sun glare.
Soon the loud plough will drive through the drifts,
Spraying it fine as white smoke,
And give the roads back. Then I'll sleep
Knowing I've seen the blizzard through.

First your papers must be put in order.
In drawer after drawer your signatures wait
To wound me. I'll let them. There's nothing else in your
    hand.
No diaries, no labelled photographs, no lists.
But here's a letter you sent one year
With my name scratched carefully on onionskin.
Empty. Man of few words, you phoned to explain.
The only letter you ever wrote me
And you posted the envelope.

No relics here of how you felt;
Maybe writing frightened you,
the way it fixed a whim.
Maybe ink and graphite made
Too rough a map of your fine love.
But remember one August night
When I was weak with fever and you held my head
And reeled off 'The Charge Of The Light Brigade'
(Of all things) to calm me. You had it by heart;
By breath. I'd hear that breath when you talked to yourself
Spitting tiny curses, or muttered in your sleep,
Or read, as monks and rabbis do, aloud, soft.

Breath that would hardly steam a mirror,
Whispering like gaslight. Day after year
After night I missed the words.

I always will. Of the funeral I recall
Only overcoats, a grey priest droning
'The letter kills,' said Paul,
'The spirit giveth life.' And my breath,
Held, jaw clamped, tight against goodbyes.

Three weeks have passed. Three weeks the clouds clenched
Low in the sky, too cold to snow until last night
When I rose to the slap of sleet on the glass and hard wind
And saw my face lamplit in the dark window,
Startled that I looked older, more like you.
Then half asleep, half frozen, close up against the pane, I
    mouthed
Father. Frost fronds quickly swirled and vanished
As if you read them back to me. Your breath
Making the blizzard silent,
The silence quiet, at last,
The quiet ours.

Cadenza

I've played it so often it's hardly me who plays.
We heard it that morning in Alexandria,
Or tried to, on that awful radio.
I was standing at the balustrade,
Watching the fish stalls opening on the quay,
The horizon already rippling in the heat.
She'd caught a snatch of Mozart, and was fishing
Through the static for the BBC
But getting bouzoukis, intimate Arabic,
All drowned beneath that soft roar, like the ocean's.
'Give it up,' I said, 'The tuner's broken.'
And then she crossed the room and kissed me. Later,
Lying in the curtained light, she whispered
She'd something to tell me. When all at once,
The tidal hiss we'd long since ceased to notice
Stopped. A flautist inhaled. And there it was,
The end of K285a,
Dubbed like a budget soundtrack on our big scene.
Next day I got the music out and learned it.

I heard it again in London a few months later,
The night she called me from the hospital.
'I've lost it,' she said, 'It happens . . .' And as she spoke
Those days in Egypt and other days returned,
Unsummoned, a tide of musics, cities, voices,
In which I drifted, helpless, disconsolate.
What did I mourn? It had no name, no sex.
'It might not even have been yours,' she said,
Or do I just imagine that she said that?

The next thing I recall, I'm in the dark
Outside St Michael's Church on Highgate Hill.
Coloured lights are strung across the portico,
Christmas lights. It's snowing on me.
And this very same cadenza – or near enough –
Rasps through a tubercular P.A.
How did I get here?

Consider that radio, drifting through frequencies,
Suddenly articulate with Mozart.
Consider the soloist playing that cadenza,
Borne to the coda by his own hands.

Lives of the artists

I The age of criticism

The clergy, who are prone to vertigo,
Dictate to heaven through a megaphone.
And those addressing Michelangelo
As he was freeing David from the stone
As much as said they thought the nose too big.
He waited till he got them on their own,
Scooped some marble dust up with his tools,
And climbing loftily atop his rig,
He tapped his chisel for those squinting fools
And let a little dust fall on their faces.

He tapped and tapped. And nothing slowly changed
Except for the opinions of Their Graces.

II The discovery and loss of perspective

Her personal vanishing point,
she said, came when she leant
against his study door
all warm and wet and whispered
Paolo. Bed.

He only muttered,
gazing down his grid, *Oh,*
what a lovely thing perspective is!
She went to live
with cousins in Madrid.

III The advance of naturalism

As any dripping clepsydra, batsqueak
In the eaves or square of angry birds,
So Donatello's steady chisel rhythm
Could sound like words. Perhaps you've read
How someone put his ear against a crack
And heard him try to make a statue speak.
Well, I was there. I heard it answer back.

Of all the cheek! it said, *Show some respect!*
The hand that makes us perfect makes us each
Submissive to the other's intellect.
Nor have we any confidence to teach
Through speaking sculpture or through sculptured speech.

Partisans

Imagine them labouring selflessly,
Gathering evidence through the long winter.
Now they bring their case before you.
'Let us arrive at the truth together.'

They say, these patient women and men.
The seconds tick by in the small cell.
The fluorescent bulb whines like a dentist's drill.
They want you to spell the names again.

Justitia

She's invisible because she's blind.
She can't be ugly. She has no face.
She will check that each confession's signed
And weigh each individual case.

She has no tongue but the final word.
She has no body. She is everyone.
It is she who bears the scales, the sword,
And noose and cattle prod and gun.

Majority

Foreign policy does not exist for us.
We don't know where the new countries are.
We don't care. We want the streets safe
So we vote for the chair. An eye for an eye.

Our long boats will come in the spring
And we will take many heads.
The name of our tribe means 'human being'.
We will make your children pray to our god in public.

Reliquary

The robot camera enters the Titanic
And we see her fish-cold nurseries on the news;
The toys of Pompeii trampled in the panic;
The death camp barrel of baby shoes;

The snow that covered up the lost girl's tracks;
The scapular she wore about her neck;
The broken doll the photojournalist packs
To toss into the foreground of the wreck.

Footage from the interior

I

Boyoko is teaching me to wait.
We squat behind wrist-thick
Stalks of palm and listen
For the faint drumming of engines.

Just after sundown
The trawler slides around the headland.
The motor coughs, whinnies and stops.
We watch and wait

As one by one the running lights
Go out across the dark lagoon.
Voices carry from the deck across the still water.
Not the words, but the sweep and glide of words.

Theirs is a tongue of tones and cadences
And Boyoko knows from the rhythm alone
Whether to slip away unseen
Or wait for rifles.

II

Boyoko is teaching me Lekele.
Our word for lagoon
Can also mean poison, or promise,
Depending on the syllable stressed.

A blue moth thrums
The windscreen of the idling jeep,
Slamming its tiny head against the glass
In urgent Morse.

Boyoko beats the word freedom
On the steering wheel.
Try it. I try it.
No, he tells me, *You said 'bacon'.*

III

Boyoko's been teaching me the 'talking drums'.
Side by side, we stand among the chickens
In the yard behind his hut.
I'm roasting. And my fingers ache.

Today when his son walked past
Boyoko lost me, slapping rhythm
Over rhythm. I stopped, he smiled
And we resumed our lesson.

Minutes passed,
And then the boy came back
Bringing two cans of cold brown beer.

Pornography

The bodies of giants shine before us like a crowded fire.
One might quite credibly shout 'Theatre'.
I can't watch this. Instead, I'll stare at the projector beam
The smoke and dust revolve in and reveal.

     Remember my story?
How one grey dawn in Maine I watched from my car
As a goshawk dove straight down toward the pines?
I said the dive was there before the hawk was,
Real as a wind shear before the blown snow reveals it.
The hawk became its aim, made one smooth purchase
In a splintering of twigs. A hare squealed, and I watched the
    bird
Slam the air in vain till it gave up and dropped its catch,
I told you how I sat and watched the rabbit die,
And described blood steaming on the frosted gravel.

     Remember how angry you were
When I told you I'd made it up?
That I'd never been to Maine or owned a car?
But I told my tale well, bought your pity for the hare,
Terror for the hawk, and I served my point,
Whatever it was.

     And remember that time
I was trapped in a cave and saw shadows on the limestone
    wall?
When the scouts freed me and carried me to the cave mouth
The true light burnt my eyes like acid. Hours passed
Before I found myself safe in the Maine woods, resting in
    my car.

THE END is near. The final frame of 'Triumph of the Will'
Slips past the lens and the blank flash blinds us.

Auto-da-fé

Last night I met my uncle in the rain
And he told me he'd been dead for fifty years.
My parents told me he'd been shot in Spain
Serving with the Irish volunteers.
But in this dream we huddled round a brazier
And passed the night in heated argument.
'*El sueño de razon . . .*' and on it went.
And as he spoke he rolled a cigarette
And picked a straw and held it to an ember.
The shape his hand made sheltering the flame
Was itself a kind of understanding.
But it would never help me to explain
Why my uncle went to fight for Spain,
For Christ, for the *Caudillo*, for the King.

Ramon Fernandez?

I met him when I fought in the brigade,
In Barcelona, when the people had it.

Red flags snapped above the tower clock
Of what had been renamed the 'Lenin Barracks'.
The ancient face was permanently fixed,
If memory serves, at half eleven.
Dead right twice a day.

Fernandez played guitar each day at noon
In the plaza beneath the barracks tower,
Hawking his revolutionary broadsides.
And as he sang he stared up at the clock
As if he half expected it to move.

I recall the way he played the crowd
Sure as he played his lacquered blue guitar.
I recall the troop trains pulling from the station,
White knuckles over carbines, boys' voices
Singing the anthems of Ramon Fernandez.

And I wonder if anyone caught on but me.
The songs the fascists sang across the wire
Were his, the same he sang, got us to sing.
A few words changed, not many. *Libertad*,
Hermana Libre, I have them all by heart.

One day he vanished back across the front
And later, when the town was under siege,
A stray round hit the barracks clock and cracked
Both iron hands clean off but left the face
To glare like a phase of the moon above the burning city.

Shibboleth

One didn't know the name of Tarzan's monkey.
Another couldn't strip the cellophane
From a GI's pack of cigarettes.
By such minutiae were the infiltrators detected.

By the second week of battle
We'd become obsessed with trivia.
At a sentry point, at midnight, in the rain,
An ignorance of baseball could be lethal.

The morning of the first snowfall, I was shaving,
Staring into a mirror nailed to a tree,
Intoning the Christian names of the Andrews Sisters.
'Maxene, LaVerne, Patti.'

Andrew Motion

In the attic

Even though we know now
your clothes will never
be needed, we keep them,
upstairs in a locked trunk.

Sometimes I kneel there,
touching them, trying to relive
time you wore them, to remember
the actual shape of arm and wrist.

My hands push down between
hollow, invisible sleeves,
hesitate, then take hold
and lift:

a green holiday; a red christening;
all your unfinished lives
fading through dark summers,
entering my head as dust.

Anniversaries

The fourth

Anniversary weather: I drive
under a raw sunset, the road
cramped between drifts, hedges
polished into sharp crests.

I have it by heart now;
on this day in each year
no signposts point anywhere
but east into Essex,

and so to your ward,
where snow recovers tonight
the ground I first saw lost
four winters ago.

Whatever time might bring,
all my journeys take me
back to this dazzling dark:
I watch my shadow ahead

plane across open fields,
out of my reach for ever,
but setting towards your bed
to find itself waiting there.

The first

What I remember is not
your leaving, but your not
coming back – and snow
creaking in thick trees,

burying tracks preserved
in spiky grass below.
All afternoon I watched
from the kitchen window

a tap thaw in the yard,
oozing into its stiff sack,
then harden when evening
closed with ice again.

And I am still there,
seeing your horse return
alone to the open stable,
its reins dragging behind

a trail across the plough,
a blurred riddle of scars
we could not decipher then,
and cannot heal now.

The second

I had imagined it all –
your ward, your shaved head,
your crisp scab stuck there
like an ornament,

but not your stillness.
Day after day I saw
my father leaning forward
to enter it, whispering

'If you can hear me now,
squeeze my hand', till snow
melted in sunlight outside
then turned to winter again

and found him waiting still,
hearing the slow hiss
of oxygen into your mask,
and always turning to say

'Yes, I felt it then',
as if repeating the lie
had gradually made it true
for him, never for you.

The third

Three years without sight,
speech, gesture, only
the shadow of clouds
shifting across your face

then blown a world away.
What sleep was that, which
light could never break?
What spellbound country

claimed you, forbidding you
even to wake for a kiss?
If it was death,
whose hands were those

warm in my own, and whose
astonishing word was it
that day when leaving
your sunlit room I heard

'Stay; stay', and watched
your eyes flick open once,
look, refuse to recognize
my own, and turn away?

The fourth

The evening falls with snow
beginning again, halving
the trees into whiteness,
driving me with it towards

the end of another year.
What will the next one bring
that this has abandoned?
You are your own survivor,

giving me back the world
I knew, without the time
we've lost. Until I forget
whatever it cannot provide

I'll always arrive like this,
having no death to mourn,
but rather the life we share
nowhere beyond your room,

our love repeating itself
like snow I watch tonight,
which spins against my window
then vanishes into the dark.

Anne Frank huis

Even now, after twice her lifetime of grief
and anger in the very place, whoever comes
to climb these narrow stairs, discovers how
the bookcase slides aside, then walks through
shadow into sunlit rooms, can never help

but break her secrecy again. Just listening
is a kind of guilt: the Westerkirk repeats
itself outside, as if all time worked round
towards her fear, and made each stroke
die down on guarded streets. Imagine it —

three years of whispering and loneliness
and plotting, day by day, the Allied line
in Europe with a yellow chalk. What hope
she had for ordinary love and interest
survives her here, displayed above the bed

as pictures of her family; some actors;
fashions chosen by Princess Elizabeth.
And those who stoop to see them find
not only patience missing its reward,
but one enduring wish for chances

like my own: to leave as simply
as I do, and walk at ease
up dusty tree-lined avenues, or watch
a silent barge come clear of bridges
settling their reflections in the blue canal.

Bathing at Glymenopoulo

Lotus eating. I can believe it:
first moment ashore the heat
stunned us – a lavish blast
and the stink of horses.
Then it was *Mister. Mister.*
Captain McKenzie – bathing girls
round from the beach, white
towels and parasols weaving
through gun-carriages, crates
and saddlery lined on the quay
to pelt us with flowers. *Want*
Captain McKenzie? I give you
good times. But we rode away,
eyes-front and smiling, pursued
until the Majestic gates.

Men to the grounds, officers
one to a cool high-ceilinged room –
mine with a balcony looking
down to the lake. There were pelicans
clambering carefully in and out
and in, never still, wrecking
the stagnant calm, fighting,
and shaking their throats
with a flabby rattle. Otherwise,
peace – the cedar layered
in enormous green-black slabs
and shading tents on the lawn;
the horses only a rumour –
stamping and snorting
out by the kitchen garden.

Early each morning we rode
to Christmas Hill – two hours
of dressage in dusty circuits
then home with the sun still low.
For the rest, time was our own;
no orders, no news from France,
but delicious boredom: polo
some evenings, and long afternoons
bathing at Glymenopoulo. Iras,
I have you by heart, giggling
and stumbling up from the breakers
into my photograph, one thin hand
pressed to your cheek, your knee-
length, navy-blue costume puckered
and clinging. I singled you out

day after day after day –
to swim with, to dawdle with
arm in arm on the beach
as the sun disappeared, and later
to hear your pidgin whispers
dancing in waterfront cafés:
*You not like anyone. Gentler
than other Captain McKenzies.
You not like the others –*
your lemony hair
loose and brushing my mouth,
your bracelets clinking,
and languorous slow waltzes
twirling us round and round
in the smoky half-light. *Luck.*

I told myself. *Luck.*
It will end – but the lazy days
stretched into months,
and then we were riding out

on a brilliant morning
to Christmas Hill as ever,
and half-way, at Kalia,
stopped at our watering place –
a date-grove fringing the pool,
the whole platoon fanned out
in a crescent to drink.
I was dismounted, leading my horse
over sugary sand, empty-headed
and waving flies from my face
when the firing began. Ten shots,

perhaps – flips and smacks
into date-trunks and nobody hurt.
But we charged –
all of us thinking *At last. Action
at last*, as our clumsy light brigade
wheeled past the trees and away
up a steady slope. I was far left,
drawing my sword with a stupid
high-pitched yelp as we laboured
through silver mirage lakes.
They were waiting ahead –
Senussi, no more than a dozen,
their gypsy silhouettes crouching
and slinking back into stones
as we breasted the rise.

The end of the world. A sheer
wall falling hundreds of feet
to a haze of yellow scrub.
I wrenched myself round, sword
dropped, head low, to a dead
teetering halt as our line
staggered, and buckled, and broke
in a clattering slide. I can

hear it again – the panicking
whinnies, shouts, and the rush
of scree where they shambled off
into space. It has taken three days
to bury them – one for the trek
to the valley floor, one to scratch
their ranks of graves, one to return.

There is little the same. At six
we have curfew now: I am writing this
after dark on my knee in the School
of Instruction grounds, in a tent.
I cannot sleep. Sirens disturb me,
groaning up from the harbour.
Those are the ships from Gallipoli,
unloading their trail of stretchers
to the Majestic, where you will be
waiting, Iras, I know, stopped
outside the gates, high-heeled
just as you were, with your hair
fluffed out after swimming:
Want Captain McKenzie?
I give you. I give you good times.

The letter

If I remember right, his first letter.
Found where? My side-plate perhaps,
or propped on our heavy brown tea-pot.
One thing is clear – my brother leaning
across asking *Who is he?* half-angry
as always that summer before enlistment.

Then alone in the sunlit yard, mother
unlocking a door to call *Up so early?*
– waving her yellow duster goodbye
in a small sinking cloud. The gate creaks
shut and there in the lane I am running
uphill, vanishing where the woodland starts.

The Ashground. A solid contour swept
through ripening wheat, and a fringe
of stippled green shading the furrow.
Now I am hardly breathing, gripping
the thin paper and reading *Write to me.*
Write to me please. I miss you. My angel.

Almost shocked, but repeating him line
by line, and watching the words jitter
under the pale spidery shadows of leaves.
How else did I leave the plane unheard
so long? But suddenly there it was –
a Messerschmitt low at the wood's edge.

What I see today is the window open,
the pilot's unguarded face somehow
closer than possible. Goggles pushed up,

a stripe of ginger moustache, and his eyes
fixed on my own while I stand
with the letter held out, my frock blowing,

before I am lost in cover again,
heading for home. He must have banked
at once, climbing steeply until his jump
and watching our simple village below –
the Downs swelling and flattening, speckled
with farms and bushy chalk-pits. By lunch

they found where he lay, the parachute
tight in its pack, and both hands spread
as if they could break the fall. I still
imagine him there exactly. His face pressed
close to the sweet-smelling grass. His legs
splayed wide in a candid unshameable V.

The dancing hippo

In my country we are not good to animals.
A dog is a dog, however it might sit up
and beg, or run through fire; and a bear
riding a bicycle still wants to eat you.
I think you can see from my lack of illusion
I have some experience – so when I tell you
this story caused me distress, do not ignore me.

It's difficult, teaching a hippo to dance.
It takes for ever. They don't grow on trees,
and buying one meant that our modest circus
made do with a mothy lion for an extra year
and sold two singing seals. Then when she arrived,
our hippo, she ate like a creature possessed –
and the shitting! Continual diarrhoea, and her tail
dithering frantically, spraying it everywhere.
I have to admit, I wanted her sold at once,
or turned into curio waste-paper baskets.

But Nikolai reckoned she'd learn. Day after day,
and sometimes night after night, we'd hear
the Dance of the Sugar Plum Fairy (with whip
obbligato) twittering out of his tent, and *Move!*
Move! while he hopped around on the straw
as if it were burning his feet. A hippo able to judge
would have certainly thought he was mad; so it may,
I suppose, have been pity that led her to copy him –
a ponderous sideways prance, a shuffling reverse,
and a massive triumphant collapse (her curtsy).

Or that's what it looked like, at least,
the first time she danced for the public –

on a summer night in some one-horse place
we found by chance in the foothills,
with warm, mosquito-y, hop-smelling air blowing in
under the rolled-up flaps, and the people
caught in the spotlight transfixed by the prance,
reverse and collapse that we thought was nothing
but seemed to them like a miracle.

Maybe it was. For sure everyone loved her,
even when summer was over, and we returned
to perform in our permanent home, in the capital,
where they are used to marvels. On opening night
under the stars in the park, she excelled herself
in front of the President, rising at one time
(I think) on her chubby back legs for a second.
Afterwards Nikolai said she was not for this world
for long, and although he was right, his philosophy
wasn't enough to prevent the fire that burst
through her pen one night in the early new year,
and burnt her to death, from breaking his heart.

We live in a country where animals count for little,
as I have said. But I remember him stumbling into my van
after the flames were doused, and the huge carcass
had gone wherever it went, gripping my arm,
leaning close to my face in the yellow glare
of my rickety kerosene lamp, and saying
I know it was useless, of course, her dancing.
I know. But God above it was beautiful.
Beautiful! God! – or something like that.

'This is your subject speaking'
In memory of Philip Larkin

On one of those evenings
which came out of nowhere,
and one drink led to another,
and then to another,

at well past midnight
(rain stinging the window,
the gas fire burbling)
you suddenly asked me:

If you could meet one poet
– they could be living or dead –
which one would you choose?
Partly to please you I told you

Hardy. *Hardy!*
All he would say is: Motion?
One of the Essex Motions perhaps?
Then came your candid guffaw,

and just for a second or so
before I laughed too,
I heard the gramophone arm
we'd forgotten, still slithering

round and round on a record,
steadily brushing the label
and filling the room with a heartbeat:
bump; bump; bump; bump; bump.

*

East of Hull, past the fishdocks,
the mile after mile of raw terraces,
the bulbous, rubbery-looking prison,

fields begin scrappily – the first few
spotted with derelict cars and sheds,
but settling gradually into a pattern:

a stunted hedge; a dead flat expanse
of plough or tussocky grass; another hedge;
another vast expanse; and nowhere

under the leisurely, washed-out clouds
a single thing to disturb the rhythm
until, like a polaroid slowly developing,

there is the spire at Patrington –
a fretted tent-pole supporting
the whole weight of the sky.

I told you about it, thinking
your church-going days long gone
and anyway never spent here,

but *Yes*, you said. *The Queen of Holderness*,
and closed your eyes – seeing yourself,
I suppose, as I see you now:

the new librarian fresh from Belfast,
pedalling off one summery Saturday
(sandwiches packed in your pockets,

grey raincoat tied on the pannier),
finding the church, standing transfixed
by knots of lushly carved stone

in the nave's subterranean light,
hearing the tired clock, and feeling
that somehow no one had seen this before

or would do again, but nevertheless
convinced it would always be safe:
a shell as withdrawn as the mind,

where apart from the weary clock,
and wind rushing the leaded glass,
there was only the sound of your footsteps

clicking the wet green flagstones,
stopping, then clicking onwards again
as you finished your slow, irregular circle.

*

There was that lunchtime
you strode from the library
half-grinning, half-scowling,
on to the Great White Way.

Would you believe it –
(your head craned down,
your office windows behind
bulging with long net curtains) –

*I'm reading the new Barbara Pym
and she says what a comfort
poetry is, when you're grieving*
(but you were laughing):

*'a poem by T. S. Eliot;
a passage by Thomas Hardy;
a line by Philip Larkin . . .' a line . . .
and think what I did for her!*

*

One particular night
you were prowling in front of my fireplace
half an eye on your drink, half on supper,

and in the mantelpiece litter of postcards,
ornaments, bowls of odourless pot-pourri,
discovered a bookmark: 'Some say

Life's the thing, but I prefer reading.'
Jesus Christ, what balls! You slewed
round on your heel to the table

almost before your anger took hold.
Later, carefully pushing your glass
through the elaborate debris of napkins

and plates shoved any old how
(so it seemed you were making a move
in chess, or planning a battle):

You see, there's nothing to write
which is better than life itself, no matter
how life might let you down, or pass you by,

and smiled – a sad, incredulous smile
which disallowed everything you or anyone
listening then might have wanted to add.

*

. . . but then again,
I'm really not surprised to be alone.
'My wife and I have asked a crowd of craps'
and 'Keep it all off'

put paid to invitations, I can tell you.
Though there was the time——
(you made a fierce deleting bleep)
wrote: 'Philip, I've to be in Hull

from February second for a day or so;
I'll get to you at half past six.'
What could I do? I had a spare room
but no furniture. So out I went

and spent a fortune on a bed,
a bedside table, chest of drawers,
a looking-glass, 'that' (you grinned)
'that vase'. Anyway, he came and went,

and then a second letter: 'My dear Philip,
wonderful to see you looking well. Thank you
for your hospitality, and jazz, and drink,
and talk.' But not a word about the furniture.

*

Now look at this.
We were stooped side by side
to a glass display-case in the library.

Two poems in two days. 'Forget What Did'
and then 'High Windows'. No corrections!
Well, not many . . .

Your writing ran
across the dark reflection of your face
in lolloping excited lines. *Don't ask me*

why I stopped. I didn't stop. It stopped.
In the old days I'd go home at six
and write all evening on a board

across my knees. But now . . . I go home
and there's nothing there. I'm like a chicken
with no egg to lay. Your breath swarmed

in a sudden fog across the glass,
cleared, and showed you staring down
a second longer, reading through the lines

then straightening. *Not bad. But that's enough
of that* (one hand sternly guiding me away).
Come on. This is someone's subject speaking.

*

*PS
You know that new anthology?
The one that Mary Wilson edited
– the favourite poems of the famous?*

*Have you seen it?
Callaghan and Mrs T and I
all chose Gray's Elegy.
Why wasn't I Prime Minister?*

*

The last place we met
*(If I'm lucky I'll know
which is the last;*

unlucky, I mean)
was the Nursing Home:
golden afternoon light,

a hot boxed-in corridor
tiled with lime-green carpet,
the door to your room ajar

and you in your linen suit
watching the Test on telly.
In the silence after applause

or laconic reports, your voice
was the cold, flat voice
of someone describing someone

they hardly knew.
Nobody's said what's wrong
and I haven't asked. Don't you.

Well I've nothing to live for,
have I? Christ, don't answer.
You'll tell me I have. Like seeing

Becker at Wimbledon, winning.
He looked just like young Auden.
That was good. I'm sure I'll die

when I'm as old as my father.
Which gives me until Christmas.
I simply can't cheer up —

and don't you start.
And don't you go, please, either,
till after my exercise . . .

Like skaters terrified their ice
might crack, we shuffled round
the dazzling patch of lawn

and fed each other lines:
how warm it was; how fast
the daisies grew; how difficult

low branches on an apple tree
made reaching the four corners —
anything which might slow down

the easy journey
to your room, the corridor again,
and then the glass front door.

The trouble is, I've written
scenes like this so many times
there's nothing to surprise me.

But that doesn't help one bit.
It just appals me. Now you go.
I won't come out. I'll watch you.

So you did: both hands lifted
palms out, fingers spread –
more like someone shocked

or fending something off
in passive desperation
than like someone waving –

but still clearly there,
and staring through the door
when I looked from my car,

waved back, pulled out,
then quickly vanished
down an avenue of sycamores

where glassy flecks of sunlight
skittered through the leaves, falling
blindingly along the empty street.

Look

I pull back the curtain
and what do I see
but my wife on a sheet
and the screen beside her
showing our twins
out of their capsule
in mooning blue,
their dawdlers' legs
kicking through silence
enormously slowly,
while blotches beneath them
revolve like the earth
which will bring them to grief
or into their own.

I pull back the curtain
and what do I see
but my mother asleep,
or at least not awake,
and the sheet folded down
to show me her throat
with its wrinkled hole
and the tube inside
which leads to oxygen
stashed round her bed,
as though any day now
she might lift into space
and never return
to breathe our air.

I pull back the curtain
and what do I see

but the stars in the sky,
and their jittery light
stabbing through heaven
jabs me awake
from my dream that time
will last long enough
to let me die happy,
not yearning for more
like a man lost in space
might howl for the earth,
or a dog for the moon
with no reason at all.

One who disappeared

Did you ever hear me tell
of that woman whose only son
was walking the cliffs at Filey
a month after moving up here

(imagine them as strangers
new from the fug of the west,
and keen to snuff up air
blasting straight out of Russia)?

If you did, then you'll have heard
how he footed the tufty edge
like a drunk walking a line,
pompously,

proud to think himself sober,
and how the smothering thump
of waves bursting in caves
drowned his giggly shout

when he floated up in a paw
of wind ripping over the cliff
like stubble-fire through a hedge
and immediately dropped away

as if he was young Mr Punch
whipped from a bare stage
and falling a hundred feet
on sheets of black rock.

*

Our boy is ill,
When I loom above

his panting hush
he scalds my face.

I look and look
and he's always there
on his soaked pallet.
I look once more

and see the woman
who watches her son
for the millionth time
in his final second

snatching a handful
of slivery grass
from the chalk fringe
then leaving her

gaping,
clenching his fists
in the salt air
as hard on nothing

as I grip your hand
when you tiptoe in
and side by side
we gaze down

at our boy in silence,
like nervous spies
in an enemy country,
marooned on a beach

waiting for rescue,
scanning the sea
for the wink of a light
which is hours overdue.

*

I'm awake to a thrush
doodling with its voice,
to the scratchy fuss of sparrows,
to a blackbird chinking loose change,

and day swirls into the street
like milk billowed through tea –
a big light lightening nothing
as it colours the map of mountains

which is you beside me, sleeping,
that muzzy gap (the door),
and through it the luminous stripes
of the cot, lurching and snuffling.

Why do I feel that I've died
and am lingering here to haunt you?
Why don't I say your name?
Why don't I touch you?

I don't even feel I'm alive
when I hear the padded thwack
of the boy kicking round in his cot –
a soft crash, like the noise

of a splintered spar of wood
which falls in the night for no reason
a long way away in a builder's yard,
then is utterly still on the moonlit cement.

A blow to the head

On the metro,
two stops in from Charles de Gaulle,
somebody slapped my wife.

Just like that –
a gang of kids –
for moving her bag
from the seat to her lap:
a thunderclap
behind my back.

Very next thing
was reeling dark
and the kids outside
beside themselves:
You didn't see! You didn't see!
It might be him! It wasn't me!

For the rest,
she wept through every station into Paris,
her head on my shoulder like love at the start of its life.

*

By the merest chance
I had in mind
J. K. stephen,
who damaged his head
on a visit to Felix-
stowe (Suffolk) in '86.

The nature of the accident is not certainly known;
in the Stephen family it was said he was struck
by some projection from a moving train.

Not a serious blow,
but it drove him mad
(molesting bread
with the point of a sword;
seized with genius –
painting all night),

and finally killed him
as well as his father,
who two years later
surrendered his heart
with a definite crack
like a sla . . .

                    *

. . . which reminds me.
When I was a kid
a man called Morris
slapped my face
so crazily hard
it opened a room
inside my head
where plates of light
skittered and slid
and wouldn't quite
fit, as they were
meant to, together.

It felt like the way,
when you stand between mirrors,
the slab of your face
shoots backwards and forwards
for ever and ever
with tiny delays,
so if you could only

keep everything still
and look to the end
of the sad succession,
time would run out
and you'd see yourself dead.

*

There is an attic flat
with views of lead
where moonlight rubs
its greasy cream,

and a serious bed
where my darling wife
lies down at last
and curls asleep.

I fit myself
along her spine
but dare not touch
her breaking skull,

and find my mother
returns to me
as if she was climbing
out of a well:

ginger with bruises,
hair shaved off,
her spongy crown
is ripe with blood.

I cover my face
and remember a dog
in a reeking yard
when the kid I was

came up to talk.
I was holding a choc
in a folded fist,
but the dog couldn't tell

and twitched away –
its snivelling whine
like human fear,
its threadbare head

too crankily sunk
to meet my eye
or see what I meant
by my opening hand.

It is an offence

The man in the flats opposite keeps a whippet
(once a racer) and two or three times a week
it craps by my front door – sloped, weary turds
like a single file of slugs in battle fatigues
(surprisingly slow for a whippet) – so that often
my shoes, my wife's, our children's bring it back home
to the stairs, the skirting, the carpets, the kitchen tiles
in bobbles or flakes or hanks or outrageous slithery smears.

The sad old dog doesn't know what he's doing, and yet
I'd still like to cover his arsehole with quick-set cement.

I admit that I also yearn to leave my mark on society,
and not see machines or people trample it foolishly.

On the one hand it's only shit; on the other, shit's shit,
and what we desire in the world is less, not more, of it.

Close

The afternoon I was killed
I strolled up the beach from the sea
where the big wave had hit me,
helped my wife and kids
pack up their picnic things,
then took my place in the car
for the curving journey home
through almost-empty lanes.

I had never seen the country
looking so beautiful –
furnace red in the poppies
scribbled all over the fields;
a darker red in the rocks
which sheltered the famous caves;
and pink in the western sky
which bode us well for tomorrow.

Nobody spoke about me
or how I was no longer there.
It was odd, but I understood why:
when I had drowned I was only
a matter of yards out to sea
(not *too far out* – too close),
still able to hear the talk
and have everything safe in view.

My sunburned wife, I noticed,
was trying to change for a swim,
resting her weight on one leg
as if she might suddenly start
to dance, or jump in the air,

but in fact snaking out of her knickers –
as shy as she was undressing
the first time we went to bed.

The Prague milk bottle

for Ivo Smoldas

The astrological clock
produces its twelve apostles
every hour

in a brainless, jerking parade
as windows wheeze open and shut,
Death twitches,

bells ping, and the cockerel crows
like a model train at a crossing
while I

get drunk in the sunlit square with Ivo
surrounded by skirts as if nothing is wrong
except:

my bath plug won't fill the hole,
my water is cold,
my phone call to home never works,
the exchange rate is shit,

and the milk!

– the milk of kindness, our mother's milk,
comes in a thing of French design,
looks like a condom and leaks like a sieve
and keeps us screaming most of the time.

*

In your wildest dreams you might whistle
and two ravens would flit their dark forest
for a baroque room you know is the British Embassy
(it has a view of Prague unmatched except by the Palace).

The ravens turn into girls and are painfully beautiful,
leaning with bare arms entwined,
black dresses crushed to the back of a yellow sofa
to take in the city you never expected to see from this angle:

miraculous spires; ecstatic saints shattered by God;
and cobbled streets where the girls will squirm in your palm
then fold into wings and fly off with a gasp –
the sound of you waking alone in your dark hotel.

*

It's not suppression,
it's humiliation.

The men they put in power
(they aren't stupid) – some of them
can hardly speak a sentence.

It's not suppression,
it's humiliation.

I have a headache. Nothing much,
but threatening to be worse – a tension
like the silence in a clock before it strikes.

It's not suppression,
it's humiliation.

My chemist writes prescriptions
but we have no drugs. I wish him ill.
None of this has much to do with girls.

It's not suppression,
it's humiliation.

*

I leave Ivo to himself
and two hours later

he's outside the airport
hoisting a bag
of toys for my children.

It's like seeing the ghost
of a friend whose death
made you say everything
there was to say.
Now there is nothing.

The milk of kindness
floods our eyes,
or maybe it's grit
swirled on the tarmac
in tottering cones.

We nod goodbye
where Security starts
and men in gloves
count my balls,
then I slither away

down a dingy tunnel
and turn again
to Ivo pinned
on a block of light
the size of a stamp,

his mechanical arm
glumly aloft,
his mouth ajar
to show he is screaming
if I could just hear.

Spring 1989

Tamworth

Red brick on red brick.

A boiled eye in a greenhouse.

Lilac smoking in sere gutters and crevices.

A missing girl's head on lamp-post after lamp-post.

*

We had taken my mother's estate
and driven into the blue –
she was in hospital then,
and didn't care.

*

Out of nowhere, nowhere else to go,
stuck in the dead afternoon, collapsed,

the mushroom hush of the lounge bar oozing up
through bilious carpet into our bed,

while men in the country nearby poked long rods
in voluptuous hedgerows, streams, rush-clumps,

fidgeting over the cracked hillsides shouting
She's not here, flinching at shadows, cursing.

*

We'd zigzagged over the map
seeing cathedral cities –
any excuse had done
to get us a week alone.

That evening under Southwell's
swarthy prolific leaves
an imp in a fissure of oak
might have been Robin Hood.

*

It was not for us. It was death –
though the men came back empty-handed
and stacked their long poles in the yard.

They understood when we packed and paid.
There were other towns, sure – plenty,
if we could hurry – our last hour of day

squeezed by a storm fuming from Nottingham way:
pitch, lemon-yellow, beech-green,
champing till ready, flighting a few big blobs

as the dusty country we entered
braced itself – leaf-hands grasping,
toads under stones, mercury ponds blinking.

*

We'd kitted out the car
with a mattress in the back,
and a sort of gyppo curtain
exactly for nights like this.

Before we left the outskirts
we posted my mother a card,
knowing my father would read it
stooping above her bed:

Fantastic carving at Southwell!
The car's going a bomb!
Not one puncture yet!
The back's really comfy!

The thing we did – the thing anyone like us did –
was find ourselves lost and be glad of it,
chittering to and fro in a lane-labyrinth
with its centre a stubble bank at the head of a valley.

Therefore we went no further. Therefore we simply sat
and watched the sky perform: elephant clouds at first
with their distant wobble and bulge like ink underwater,
then splits of thunder, then the sour flash of light

glancing off metal, then clouds with their hair slicked back,
edgy, crouching to sprint, and when sprinting at last
fanned flat, guttering, flicking out ochre tongues
before losing their heads altogether, boiled down

to a Spanish skirt cartwheeling through woods,
a heavy boot squelching out squall after squall
of leaf-mould, nail, hair, and Christ knows what
shrieks and implorings we never caught even a word of.

*

We burrowed against each other
after the storm had gone,
and saw between our curtains
lightning over the valley

on its nimble silver legs –
one minute round our car,
the next high up in heaven
kicking splinters off stars –

then skipping away to somewhere
with the thunder-dog behind it
grumbling but exhausted,
and leaving us such silence

I'd swear I heard the moon
creak as it entered the sky,
and the stubble field around us
breathing earth-smell through its bristles.

Dedication

In broad daylight and a familiar street –
the sort where gossips dawdle and nose-to-tail dogs meet –

some bastard with no face lurched out from behind a tree
and tried to kill me.

There was tooth-flash, black leather, the smile of a knife
and I saw the terrified puffed-out bird of my life

fly from my hand – so for a long second I knew I was dead
even though I was still fighting him off, even though I'd just
    said

No! No! and then in a flurried muddle *Go on! Go on!*
(meaning all I most wanted to do in the world had hardly
    begun)

before my heart started working again and I stood there
    alone
dribbling a little thin blood from one finger on to a ringing
    paving-stone.

*

I thought that was all
but then night fell

and the knife became
an adder's tongue

bitterly licking me,
slicing easily,

down and down
through my open brain

until all I'd begun,
half-finished, done,

or wished to be true
was gone. All except you.

*

But you were asleep and made no sound
when I left your side without a word

and slipped away to my basement room,
a grown man like a frightened child.

The fire is out at the heart of the world;
all tame creatures have grown up wild.

The lives I trusted, even my own,
collapse, break off or don't belong.

I leant my head on the window-pane
and the hard-edged garden, lit with rain,

shimmered a million knives; the wind
caressed them with its painful hand.

The fire is out at the heart of the world;
all tame creatures have grown up wild —

all except you, your life like a cloud
I am lost in now and will never be found.

A dream of peace

It starts like this
with stick or stone
or sharpened bone

and a hill in the wilds
where a crotchety oak
soughs over a cave

and the face of fire
flares all day
all night all day

and *clink clinkety clink*
might be the hammer
of something new

or might be a bird
buried deep in the oak
which sings its heart out

with nothing to say
except what happens
to strike home next.

*

It starts like that and it comes to this:
my father's tank – *clank clankety clank* –
just one of hundreds, sprigged with leaves,
on a rippling road through northern France,

and blossoming light on apple trees,
and singing larks like dots in the sun,
and easy climbs and the summer wind,
and the . . .

*

In a twinkling the sun has vanished behind a barn, then it is
out again. A moment ago he would have sworn everything
looked like home – like Essex! But when he turns off the road
into a field it is not like Essex at all. On the bank of a stream
is a soldier's fair-haired head with no jaw to it, no mouth. This
is all he can find.

*

I wanted a big language for the people who died –
I wanted a big language for fighting. I found one,
but only when peace descended; then I looked back
and the apple-roads, my vanished brothers-in-arms,
the ruined flickering outskirts of the capital,
a dead dog in a pram, the enormous iron station
with its roof blown off, the herded people:
all were part of my big language.
                                        I filled my lungs
and shouted until I had ripped the leaves from every tree in
     sight
and raised a creamy wave on even the smallest buried lakes.
My language had conquered the world.
I was free to say what I wanted.

*

When I was a boy at the head of the stairs
my life was the life of the senses.
I cooled my face at a window above the yard

and saw in the melting distance a second boy
who could have been just like me but was not,
flapping his arms like someone about to take off

if only he could get free of the tangling grass
and the dull weight of his shoes, and the geese
he was driving ahead in a brilliant scattering cloud.

The grass, the wet, the melting light, the geese.
It was panicky, but it had something to do with peace.

*

What should I die for?
Answer me that.
What should I live for?
Clickety clack.

Give me your answer.
Clickety clack.
Show me a war
then take it back.

*

I fell in love with a soldier
seventy years younger than me,
who knew the country best
as soon as he left it to die.

Under a beech tree in Essex
he practised how it would go,
squeezing a gun barrel into his mouth
then deciding no.

But I knew nothing of that:
I only saw a soldier
hearing how death would be
in the dry crack of branches

echoing endlessly.

*

I knew nothing, or less than nothing.
I knew books.

I knew
'Gas! Gas! Quick, boys!'
and learnt it,
saying it slowly:
'Gas! Gas! Quick, boys!'
The wrong war, the wrong speed, the wrong accent.

Nobody noticed.
In the dusty classroom
sunlight went solid with dust.
Quick! Quick!
Slow. Slow.
My tongue turned heavily over
and sank in the deepest sleep.
I knew nothing, or less than nothing.
The wrong war, the wrong speed, the wrong accent.

*

Yes, I fell in love with a soldier
seventy years younger than me,
and after I had him by heart
I went to discover his grave.
This was not being brave.

Like mirrors, like snow, like chips of ice
white stones appear outside a wood.
Quick! Quick! It will soon be dark
and I won't be able to read their names
or come here again.

His voice ran by like a wave on a buried lake,
so quiet I had to hold my breath.
There it was then! A whisper and gone –
a secret I wanted to have as my own
if I ever got home.

I dreamed a woman made me take off my ring
(my father's ring) and at once I imagined a man
who stopped by a river somewhere up north from here
and threw in a ribbon which showed how brave he was.

Then in my dream the man was smothered by smoke
and I was aloft, catching the woman (the same woman)
up in my arms so we flew like a wounded gull,
me in my black, her in a rippling wedding-dress.

The whole country spread itself open below –
towns and villages, motorways, ring roads, lanes,
water-logged moorland, grazing, a plain of wheat –
and we knew it contained whatever we meant by home.

The moon came out, and down we dipped close to the earth
where elm tops tickled the woman's defenceless feet
and we searched for the intimate, beautiful detail in things:
a marbled starling, for instance, asleep on a telephone line.

By now I was tired and knew we had left it too late;
all we could see was wire, and too many eyes,
and a big gate like a grill wherever we went,
and a searchlight we could not escape for a moment longer.

We circled and circled, helplessly caught in each other,
not like a man and a woman at all, and not like a gull,
but a frivolous smidgin of paper blown up in a fire,
which twiddles away from the earth and cannot return.

*

What language to speak
in a world apart?
How to describe
peace in a heart?

My tongue woke up
but could not speak.
I opened my mouth:
clink clinkety clink.

*

They kept on jumping up, their happiness like a trampoline,
and set to at once. Chunks came away, rare as moon rock, or
fragments spiky with thick brown wire, or a whole door-shaped
section blurted over with writing. You couldn't read what it
said, no sentence came away complete, so what they carried
off were gasps and grunts.

    We slumped in our armchairs watching, my father and I,
and I wanted to know: did he recognize any of this? He shook
his head while I imagined the ruined flickering outskirts, the
enormous iron station with its roof blown off.

    'It must make you wonder?'

    'Yup', was all he would say, 'Yup', and kept on looking away.

*

Change the channel.

With our son between us
asleep and dreaming
the news floats up
in a blaring wash.

Press the button.

Now here is a soldier
who stands in the desert
and shouts a language
I do not know.

Change the channel.

Oh, but I see:
it's 'Gas! Gas! Gas!'
rattled so fast
it means nothing to me.

Press the button.

Now here is a tank
overtaken by camels –
it makes no sense.
Clank clankety clank.

Change the channel.

Oh, but I see:
the camels are leaving
the world where no one
expects to survive.

Press the button.

Now here is the nothing
we see in the dark
when pictures stop
and voices die.

Change the channel.

Oh, but I see:
it's not nothing at all –
two faces are there
in the creaking drizzle,

faint and silent,
while rising between them
the child wakes up
and cries to be fed.

Press the button.

*

There's nothing special in this goodbye at my father's house:
too much to drink, too much to eat, too many rooms too
   warm,

and the talk slowing down to traffic and the best and worst
   way home
in a language not exactly dead but not exactly loving.

So let the music start. Then comes the spurt of tyres on
   gravel.
My father turns back to his house like someone walking
   underwater.

Hugo Williams

Don't look down

Don't look down. Once
You look down you own
The fall in your heart,
You rock your stance
On the stone
And hear your ending start.

It climbs up to you
Out of a deep pit
In sentences
Half followed through
And sighs which twist it
Till it wrenches

At your hold, or shows
You as a clown
Whose imitation rage
Will draw from rows
Of seats some laughter, thrown
Like nuts into a cage.

While high in the big top
A white-clad flyer springs
And it is he you were
Who made men stop
And wonder at your wings
So famous in that air,

Until you looked down
And saw your future there
In the dust and light
And suddenly were thrown
Into that pit where
Now you trot each night.

The butcher

The butcher carves veal for two.
The cloudy, frail slices fall over his knife.

His face is hurt by the parting sinews
And he looks up with relief, laying it on the scales.

He is a rosy young man with white eyelashes
Like a bullock. He always serves me now.

I think he knows about my life. How we prefer
To eat in when it's cold. How someone

With a foreign accent can only cook veal.
He writes the price on the grease-proof packet

And hands it to me courteously. His smile
Is the official seal on my marriage.

The couple upstairs

Shoes instead of slippers down the stairs,
She ran out with her clothes

And the front door banged and I saw her
Walking crookedly, like naked, to a car.

She was not always with him up there,
And yet they seemed inviolate, like us,
Our loves in sympathy. Her going

Thrills and frightens us. We come awake
And talk excitedly about ourselves, like guests.

Sugar Daddy

You do not look like me. I'm glad
England failed to colonize
Those black orchid eyes
With blue, the colour of sun-blindness.

Your eyes came straight to you
From your mother's Martinique
Great-grandmother. They look at me
Across this wide Atlantic

With an inborn feeling for my weaknesses.
Like love-letters, your little phoney grins
Come always just too late
To reward my passionate clowning.

I am here to be nice, clap hands, reflect
Your tolerance. I know what I'm for.
When you come home fifteen years from now
Saying you've smashed my car,

I'll feel the same. I'm blood-brother,
Sugar daddy, millionaire to you.
I want to buy you things.

I bought a garish humming top
And climbed into your pen like an ape
And pumped it till it screeched for you,
Hungry for thanks. Your lip

Trembled and you cried. You didn't need
My sinister grenade, something
Pushed out of focus at you, swaying
Violently. You owned it anyway

And the whole world it came from.
It was then I knew
I could only take things from you from now on.

I was the White Hunter,
Bearing cheap mirrors for the Chief.
You saw the giving-look coagulate in my eyes
And panicked for the trees.

Family

In the bosom of the family
A court is in session.

The jury retire.
They run screaming through the streets.

Sonny Jim

In my jacket and your jewels
The pusher is always with us.
Our little Sonny Jim.
We can't take our eyes off him.

I came home one night
And he was combing his hair like a mermaid.
I hung my coat on a peg
And it looked to me like a shroud.

Jim smiled lovingly round at me,
Long teeth in a skull. I thought:
'Some secret has dissolved his eyes.'
He bridled yellowly.

Since then we take him everywhere we go.
He is a monkey on a stick.
He only talks about one thing:
Sonny Jim is his own latest trick.

The prettiest boy in his class,
He can tell you all there is
To being a speedfreak at fifteen.
He has the track on his groin.

'They make you roll up your sleeves
And your trousers. I've seen jammed
Forearms come away like plaster
When a bandage is unwound.'

We rock him in our arms
And murmur at the world we bailed him from.
Moses in the bulrushes
Was not more loved than our Sonny Jim.

February the 20th Street

A coincidence must be
Part of a whole chain
Whose links are unknown to me.

I feel them round me
Everywhere I go: in queues,
In trains, under bridges,

People, or coincidences, flukes
Of logic which fail
Because of me, because

We move singly through streets,
The last of some sad species,
Pacing the floors of zoos,

Our luck homing forever
Backward through grasses
To the brink of another time.

Pay day

'At the end of the world,' said the crone
'Are blue and red days
Wrapped and waiting in the shade
And yours for the taking.'

I set one foot on the porch.
The boards creaked. The crone
Looked up from her sleeping with a start.
'The chillies are under the cloth,' she said
'But they ain't been paid for.'

Holidays

We spread our things on the sand
In front of the hotel
And sit for hours on end
Like merchants under parasols
Our thoughts following the steamers
In convoy across the bay
While far away

Our holidays look back at us in surprise
From fishing boats and fairs
Or wherever they were going then
In their seaweed headdresses.

To my daughter

A little girl sits on the wall
Colouring something on the other side.
The wind shines her hair as she holds up
A flapping paper to my window.

What is on the paper I don't know.
The hornbeam bends over near her head.
Its two-coloured leaves are like her hair.

Tides

The evening advances, then withdraws again,
Leaving our cups and books like islands on the floor.
We are drifting you and I,
As far from one another as the young heroes
Of these two novels we have just laid down.
For that is happiness: to wander alone
Surrounded by the same moon, whose tides remind us of
    ourselves,
Our distances, and what we leave behind.
The lamp left on, the curtains letting in the light.
These things were promises. No doubt we will come back to
    them.

Impotence

You see me with my suits, my well-cut suits:
Past, present and future
Ranged close at hand upon their hooks.

How you hated them, hanging there so like me they hurt,
The herringbones, the faint chalk stripes,
Withdrawn from the wear and tear.

They were never in the wrong, the multi-pocketed,
The stay-at-homes. They were cosy-warm,
Huddling together there.

But where did you go that night
While I hung about upstairs, unwell, unable to decide,
Should I wear this one? Or that?
Take off the tie, or keep the waistcoat on?

You couldn't wait
When time ran out on me. I crossed the floor too late
To shut the cupboard which contained the sea.

Bachelors

What do they know of love,
These men who have never been married?
What do they know
About living face to face with happiness,
These amateurs of passion?
Do they imagine it's like home used to be,
Having a family of one's own,
Watching the little bones grow lethal,
The eyes turned on you –
And realizing suddenly that it's all
Your own fault the way things are,
Because it's you now,
Not your parents who're in charge?
Can they understand what it means,
These suntanned single men? Or are they into cars?

And what do they know about the bedside lamp,
These denimed Romeos,
Its sphere of influence as night descends,
Familiar switch to hand:

On-off, off-on, the thousand little clicks
Half in, half out of the dark,
As the row gets going on time, or nothing does,
Or the bulb just sings to itself
On your side of the bed?
Pride in anger. That's your happiness.
A poisonous seed washed up with you
On a desert island of your own making,
Your impotence in flower like a hothouse rose.
And they talk about love,
These men who have never been married.

Stagefright

(thinking of my father)

Dazed with the sadness of lost things
In ordered silence
I sat down in the dining-room for tea:
Biscuits and a glass of Moselle, no radio.
(How kind we are to ourselves!)
And I tried to imagine
What he would have done at a time like this
For I will say this
He knew what to do in an emergency
And he knew what to drink.
So I put some more wine in the fridge
And I hurried round to her house.
I shouted her name and knocked
But she spoke to me through the frosted glass
And I'm glad I couldn't see her face
When she told me it was all over between us.

Then I shivered like a man with stagefright
And I watched the world
Come slowly to a standstill before my eyes:
The sinking of the heart.
It seemed unacceptable suddenly
To be walking the streets on such a night
With love like so much small change
Left over from a pound.
I could hear him telling me:
'Women are strong, but they fall
Like sleep from your eyes. Let your step
Spring on the sidewalk and you'll see
Your only fault's unhappiness.'
Then I came back here and got into my good suit,
Having chucked the biscuits
And opened the bottle of wine.

Confessions of a drifter

I used to sell perfume in the New Towns.
I was popular in the saloons.
Professional women slept in my trailer.
Young salesgirls broke my heart. For ten years
I never went near our Main Office.

From shop to shop
And then from door to door I went
In a slowly diminishing circle of enchantment
With 'Soir de Paris' and 'Flower of the Orient'.

I used up all my good luck
Wetting the wrists of teenagers in bars
With 'English Rose' and 'Afro-Dizziac'
From giveaway dispensers.

From girl to girl
And then from bar to bar I went
In a slowly expanding circle
Of liquid replenishment.

I would park my trailer outside a door
So I could find it when I walked out of there,
Throwing back my shoulders at the night – a hero
To myself.

They knock on my window this morning. Too late
I wake out of my salesman's paradise,
The sperm drying on my thigh
And nothing but the name of a drifter in the New Towns.

At least a hundred words

What shall we say in our letters home?
That we're perfectly all right?
That we stand on the playground with red faces
and our hair sticking up?
That we give people Chinese burns?
Mr Ray, standing in the entrance to the lavatories
with his clipboard and pen,
turned us round by our heads
and gave us a boot up the arse.
We can't put that in our letters home
because Mr Ray is taking letter-writing.
He sits in his master's chair
winding the propeller of his balsa wood aeroplane
with a glue-caked index finger
and looking straight ahead.
RESULTS OF THE MATCH, DESCRIPTION OF THE
   FLOODS,
THE LECTURE ON KENYA, UGANDA AND TANGANYIKA
WITH COLOUR SLIDES AND HEADDRESSES.
We have to write at least a hundred words
to the satisfaction of Mr Ray
before we can go in to tea,
so I put up my hand to ask if we count the 'ands'.
Mr Ray lets go the propeller of his Prestwick 'Pioneer'
and it unwinds with a long drawn-out sigh.
He'd rather be out overflying
enemy territory on remote
than 'ministering to the natives' in backward C4.
He was shot down in World War One or World War
Two, he forgets,
but it didn't do him a damn bit of harm.

It made a man of him.
He goes and stands in the corner near the door
and offers up his usual prayer:
'One two three four five six seven
God give me strength to carry on.'
While his back is turned
I roll a marble along the groove in the top of my desk
till it drops through the ink-well
on to the track I've made for it inside. I can hear it
travelling round the system of books
and rulers: a tip-balance, then a spiral,
then a thirty-year gap as it falls through
the dust-hole into my waiting hand.

A walking gentleman

I started very slowly,
being rude to everybody
and going home early
without really knowing why.
I carried on that way
till my father died
and allowed me to grow my hair.
I didn't want to any more.
I came through a side door,
my hands slightly raised,
as if whatever was going on
needed lifting by me.
I bought a clove carnation
in Moyses Stevens

and walked all the way up Piccadilly
to the top of the Haymarket,
stopping every so often.
Surely Scott's is somewhere near here?
I can't see it any more.
My feet are hurting me.

Tipping my chair

I shivered in 1958. I caught a glimpse
of money working and I shut my eyes.
I was a love-sick crammer-candidate, reading
poetry under the desk in History,
wondering how to go about my life.
'Write a novel!' said my father.
'Put everything in! Sell the film rights for a fortune!
Sit up straight!' I sat there, filleting
a chestnut leaf in my lap, not listening.
I wanted to do nothing, urgently.

At his desk, in his dressing-gown,
among compliant womenfolk, he seemed
too masterful, too horrified by me.
He banged the table if I tipped my chair.
He couldn't stand my hair. One day,
struggling with a chestnut leaf, I fell over backwards
or the chair leg broke. I didn't care any more
if poetry was easier than prose. I lay there
in the ruins of a perfectly good chair
and opened my eyes. I knew what I didn't want to do.

At his desk, in his dressing-room, among
these photographs of my father in costume,
I wonder how to go about his life.
Put everything in? The bankruptcy? The hell?
The little cork-and-leather theatrical
'lifts' he used to wear? The blacking for his hair?
Or again: leave everything out? Do nothing,
tip my chair back and stare at him for once,
my lip trembling at forty?
My father bangs the table: 'Sit up straight!'

Tangerines

'Before the war' was once-upon-a-time
by 1947. I had to peer through cigarette smoke
to see my parents in black and white
lounging on zebra skins, while doormen stood by doors
in pale grey uniforms.

I wished I was alive before the war
when Tony and Mike rode their bicycles into the lake,
but after the war was where I had to stay,
upstairs in the nursery, with Nanny
and the rocking-horse. It sounded more fun
to dance all night and fly to France for breakfast.
But after the war I had to go to bed.

In my prisoner's pyjamas I looked through
banisters into that polished, pre-war place
where my parents lived. If I leaned out
I could see the elephant's foot

tortured with shooting sticks
and a round mirror which filled from time to time
with hats and coats and shouts,
then emptied like a bath.

Every summer my parents got in the car
and drove back through the war to the South of France.
I longed to go with them, but I was stuck
in 1948 with Nanny Monkenbeck.

They sent me sword-shaped eucalyptus leaves
and purple, pre-war flowers, pressed
between the pages of my first letters. One year
a box of tangerines arrived for me from France.
I hid behind the sofa in my parents' bedroom,
eating my way south to join them.

Now that I hear trains

Now that I hear trains
whistling out of Paddington on their way to Wales,
I like to think of him, as young as he was then,
running behind me along the sand,
holding my saddle steady
and launching me off on my own.

Now that I look unlike
the boy on the brand-new bike
who wobbled away down the beach,
I hear him telling me: 'Keep pedalling, keep pedalling.'
When I looked over my shoulder
he was nowhere to be seen.

Walking out of the room backwards

Out of work at fifty, smoking fifty a day,
my father wore his sheepskin coat
and went to auditions
for the first time in his life.
I watched in horror from my bedroom window
as he missed the bus to London
in full view of the house opposite.
'If it weren't for you and the children,'
he told my mother from his bed,
'I'd never get up in the morning.'

He wasn't amused
when I burst in on his sleep
with a head hollowed out of a turnip
swinging from a broom. There were cigarette burns
like bullet holes in his pyjamas.
I saw his bad foot
sticking out from under the bedclothes
because he was 'broke'
and I thought my father was dying.
I wanted to make him laugh, but I got it wrong
and only frightened myself.

The future stands behind us, holding ready
a chloroform-soaked handkerchief, in case we make a slip.
The past stretches ahead, into which we stare,
as into the eyes of our parents
on their wedding day –
shouting something from the crowd
or waving things on sticks

to make them look at us. To punish me,
or amuse his theatrical friends,
my father made me walk out of the room backwards,
bowing and saying, 'Goodnight, my liege.'

Scratches

My mother scratched the soles of my shoes
to stop me slipping
when I went away to school.

I didn't think a few scratches
with a pair of scissors
was going to be enough.

I was walking on ice,
my arms stretched out.
I didn't know where I was going.

Her scratches soon disappeared
when I started sliding
down those polished corridors.

I slid into class.
I slid across the hall into the changing-room.
I never slipped up.

I learnt how to skate along with an aeroplane
or a car, looking ordinary,
pretending to have fun.

I learnt how long a run I needed
to carry me as far as the gym
in time for Assembly.

I turned as I went,
my arms stretched out to catch the door jamb
as I went flying past.

Snorkel

To my brother

You carried the rattans and the towels.
I carried the wind shield
and one of the old snorkels
with ping-pong balls for valves.

What happened to the other one
with yellow glass, the one that was dangerous?
We both wanted that one.
It didn't mist up. We slung ourselves

halfway between heaven and earth
that summer – holding our breath
and diving for sand dollars.
If we breathed out all the air in our lungs

we could grab another ten seconds
on the seabed. We spent half our lives
waiting for each other to come out of the water
so we could have our turn.

The Spring of Sheep

Pro-Plus Rapid Energy Tablets
gave me Extra Vitality
when I visited my girlfriend on her father's stud.
The double-backing local bus
took two hours to travel twenty miles.
When it passed our house
I nearly got off by mistake.
I noticed a roof I hadn't been on
and I wished I was up there with my gun.
My hands were shaking
as I thought of things to say:
how the enlargements had gone astray
and been pinned to the noticeboard,
how my tutor asked if it was Brigitte Bardot.
I practised laughing in the window of the bus,
but I laughed on the other side of my face
when I saw her riding her pony
in her Sloppy Joe.
We were sitting alone in the nursery,
waiting for her father's horse to appear on television.
My left hand felt numb,
but my right took leave of its senses
and set out for the unknown regions of her shoulders.
I watched through binoculars
as it lay there with altitude sickness.
If it was mine, how could I get it back in time
for dinner with her parents, bloodstock
and doping scandals? A gong
sounded somewhere in the house
and I leapt to my feet. Everyone was proud
of the gallant Citizen Roy

and my girlfriend ran over to the stables
to say goodnight. Head-over-heels with Pro-Plus,
I lay awake for hours, experiencing fierce
but tender feelings for the mattress
in a spare room hung with antique jigsaws:
'Les Généraux en herbe (The Future Generals)'
'Le Jeu de Balle (The Game of Balls)'
'Le Saut du Mouton (The Spring of Sheep)'.

Going round afterwards

His face was orange.
His widow's peak had been blacked in.
I knew it was him,
because he didn't speak.
'Congratulations!' I said.
'I didn't know you could cry.'
His dresser was holding
a pair of check trousers
underneath his chin. He let the legs
drop through a coat-hanger
and smiled at me deafly.
'It's just a trick,' said my father.
'Anyone can do it.'
I stood there with my drink,
feeling the ingenious glamour
of being cramped, the mild delinquency
of things behind curtains –
shirts and cardigans
that should have been at home.

Did I have the guts?
And did you have to want it all that much
in order to go on?
His face came up from the wash-basin
white and unwell again,
a trace of make-up underneath his ears.
His dresser was handing him
another pair of trousers,
holding them up off the floor
as my father stepped into them.

Death of an actor

i.m. Hugh Williams 1904–1969

I

Now that I am cold
Now that I look like him
I put on this warm grey suit of wool
In sympathy with my father.

Now that I'm alone
Now that I have come to this nice
Indifference
I sweep my hair straight back
The way he wore it during his life
And after he was dead
His fierce forehead
Still doubting the intelligence
Of those who approached where he lay.

2

Now that he is dead
Now that he is remembered
Unfavourably by some
For phrases too well cut
To fit their bonhomie
I wonder what he was like
This stiff theatrical man
With his air of sealed regret.
'I'd have made a first class tramp,'
He told me once,
'If I'd had more money.'

Now that it is late
Now that it is too late
For filial piety
I can but thank him for
His bloody-mindedness.
Face expressionless with pain
He ordered me a suit in Savile Row
The very day he took
The last plunge backwards
Into secrecy and sweat.
'O Dad, can dead men swim?'

3

Gold on the doorstep, whose steps
Nag the sand drifts.
Gold in the spittoon.

My father would sit on the steps
Emptying his shoe.
Pitchers of sand on each step.

If they went on, they would lead
Nowhere. Gold in a silver spoon.
My father's throat torn to sand.

4

Our first Christmas after the war
A triangular package
Arrived from his producer.

'Greetings from Emile Littler'
Said the message printed on the bar
Of a single coat-hanger.

5

Now that I have tucked myself in
To this deep basement calm
And the windows are sealed for winter,
Now that my life is organized
To absorb the shock
Of looking back at it,
I understand why he put such vast whiskies
Into the hands of his enemies
And I take back what I said.

Now that I am grown
Now I have children of my own
To offer me their own
Disappointed obedience
I feel for him.
Our children left us both
Because we sat so still
And were too wise for them
When they told us their best jokes.

6

'My father was last to leave the stage
In *The Cherry Orchard* in 1966.
He said to his bookshelves,
My friends, my dear good friends,
How can I be silent?
How can I refrain from expressing, as I leave,
The thoughts that overwhelm my being?'
His sister was calling him,
'The station . . . the train. Uncle,
Shouldn't we be going?'

7

The recording starts too late
To drown the sound of wheels. A little screen
Jerks upwards and the coffin
Wobbles towards us on rollers, like a diving-board.
This is my father's curtain-call. His white-ringed eyes
Flicker to the gallery as he bows to us. He bows
To his leading lady, then steps back again,
Rejoining hands with the cast.

In the dressing-room afterwards
He pours us all champagne:
'It's like a madhouse here. We're staffed by chumps.
The stage manager thinks the entire production
Stems from his control panel, like a cremation.
He's never heard of laughs. As for the set,
Tom says it's the old Jermyn Street Turkish Baths
Painted shit. Let's hope it doesn't run.'

8

Now that he is gone
Now that we have followed him this far
To a push-button crematorium
In unknown Golders Green
I think how near he seems, compared to formerly,
His head thrown back like that
Almost in laughter.
I used to watch him making up
In an underground dressing-room,
His head thrown back that way:
A cream and then a bright red spot
Rubbed down to a healthy tan.

Now that he is gone
Now that we have seen his coffin
Roll through those foul flaps
And a curtain ring down for the last time
On a sizeable man
I remember how calm he remained
Throughout the final scene,
Sitting bolt upright
On a windswept platform.
'The coldest place in the south of England,'
He used to say – off on tour again
In one of his own plays.

9

Now that he has returned to that station
Where the leave-train is waiting
Blacked-out and freezing,
The smell of whisky lingers on my breath,
A patch of blue sky
Stings like a slap in the face.

Now that he isn't coming down
On the midnight train tonight, or any night,
I realize how far
Death takes men on from where they were
And yet how soon
It brings them back again.

10

Now that I'm the same age
As he was during the war,
Now that I hold him up like a mirror
To look over my shoulder,
I'm given to wondering
What manner of man it was
Who walked in on us that day
In his final uniform.
A soldier with two families?
An actor without a career?
'You didn't know who on earth I was,' he told me.
'You just burst into tears.'

Now that he has walked out again
Leaving me no wiser,
Now that I'm sitting here like an actor
Waiting to go on,
I wish I could see again
That rude, forgiving man from World War II
And hear him goading me.
Dawdling in peacetime,
Not having to fight in my lifetime, left alone
To write poetry on the dole and be happy,
I'm given to wondering
What manner of man I might be.

When I Grow up

When I grow up I want to have a bad leg.
I want to limp down the street I live in
without knowing where I am. I want the disease
where you put your hand on your hip
and lean forward slightly, groaning to yourself.

If a little boy asks me the way
I'll try and touch him between the legs.
What a dirty old man I'm going to be when I grow up!
What shall we do with me?

I promise I'll be good
if you let me fall over in the street
and lie there calling like a baby bird. Please,
nobody come. I'm perfectly all right. I like it here.

I wonder would it be possible
to get me into a National Health Hospice
somewhere in Manchester?
I'll stand in the middle of my cubicle
holding on to a piece of string for safety,
shaking like a leaf at the thought of my suitcase.

I'd certainly like to have a nervous tic
so I can purse my lips up all the time
like Cecil Beaton. Can I be completely bald, please?
I love the smell of old pee.
Why can't I smell like that?

When I grow up I want a thin piece of steel
inserted into my penis for some reason.
Nobody's to tell me why it's there. I want to guess!
Tell me, is that a bottle of old Burgundy

under my bed? I never can tell
if I feel randy any more, can you?

I think it's only fair that I should be allowed
to cough up a bit of blood when I feel like it.
My daughter will bring me a special air cushion
to hold me upright and I'll watch
in baffled admiration as she blows it up for me.

Here's my list: nappies, story books, munchies,
something else. What was the other thing?
I can't remember exactly,
but when I grow up I'll know. When I grow up
I'll pluck at my bedclothes to collect lost thoughts.
I'll roll them into balls and swallow them.

Self-portrait with a speedboat

You wouldn't think it to look at me,
but I was a hot property once upon a time
to my sponsors, Johnson and Johnson Baby Oil.

I reached the final of the 1980
World Powerboat Championship – myself,
Lucy Manners, Werner Panic and the rest.

I was going for the record
of no hours, no minutes, no seconds
and I reckoned I was in with a chance.

I was dancing the *Self-Portrait* along
inside the yellow buoys, nice dry water ahead,
when I started picking up some nonsense

from my old rival Renato Salvadori,
the knitwear salesman from Lake Como,
appearing for Martini.

Renato was chopping up the water with a series
of kick turns and yells and throwing it
in my face like a gauntlet, flak

from his tailplane running off my goggles.
I was pushing the *Self-Portrait*
into a sizeable swell, but I figured the aerofoil

would keep her nose down in an emergency,
the headrest would account for any recoil
occasioned by overdrive – 4g,

that's about four times your body weight
screwing your neck around on corners
and pinning a smile on your face.

I looked over my shoulder and saw Werner Panic
hovering and bouncing about.
The three of us hit the Guinness hairpin

at about ninety, sashaying our arses
round the corner post and spraying the customers
with soda water, which they didn't seem to mind.

You can either go into these things tight
and come out wide, or you can go in wide
and come out tight, depending on your mood.

But whereas Werner and myself went into it
tight and came out of it laughing,
Renato lost his bottle completely

and wound up pointing backwards in a pool
of engine oil, miming outrage
and holding out his hands to the judges.

His departure for Lake Como in the relief launch,
clutching his crash helmet
and lucky sombrero mascot,

left me aquaplaning the wash
from Werner's dog-leg, covert blue and gold
tobacco logo making me see red.

I'm very fond of Werner, but I'm not about to
hand him the trophy on a platter
just because he smokes Rothmans.

I sat on his coat-tails for a lap or two,
revs going from 7½ to ten thou,
big V8 engine powering along at about a hundred.

I'll never forget his face
as the *Self-Portrait* took off on his starboard wake
and entered the unofficial record books

for ski-jumping – 19 feet of aluminium
chucked in a great curve between heaven and earth –
a trajectory to nowhere as it turned out,

but I didn't know that then. As I looked down
on the scene spread out beneath me,
I remember thinking what a fabulous

powerboat atmosphere there was
on the Royal docks that afternoon –
champagne and cigars, jellied eels, a Big Top

with four shows a day, dolphins, a gorilla,
girls in pink leotards, all the fun of the fair.
As I touched down near the pits

my arm came up to say 'thank-you' to my mechanics
for making it all possible.
You can see one of them – Pasquale that is –

returning the compliment at the exact moment
the *Self-Portrait* hits the pier
of the escape basin and vanishes under a layer

of polystyrene blocks, old aerosol cans
and water-logged flyers for the 1980
World Powerboat Championship. That's me

standing up to my neck in dirty water,
holding up a shattered steering-wheel
to cheers from the salvage barge.

Desk duty

My desk has brought me
all my worst fears on a big tray
and left it across my lap.
I'm not allowed to move until I have
eaten everything up.
I push things around on my plate.
I kick the heating pipes.

A piece of worn carpet on the floor
proves how long I've been sitting here
shuffling my feet,
opening and closing drawers,
looking for something I've lost
under piles of official papers and threats,
roofing grants and housing benefits.

Am I married or single?
Employed or self-employed?
What sort of work do I do?
Is my house being used for business
or entertainment purposes? (See Note 3)
If I am resident at my place of work,
who supplies the furniture?

I have cause to suspect myself
of deliberately wasting time
writing my name and place of birth
under 'Who else lives with you?'
It has taken me all day
to find something true to write
under 'Personal Allowances' – or not untrue.

I know all about my little game
of declaring more than I earn
to the Inland Revenue – or was it less?
I'm guilty as hell,
or I wouldn't be sitting here like this
playing footy-footy with my desk.
I'd be upstairs in bed with my bed.

Toilet

I wonder will I speak to the girl
sitting opposite me on this train.
I wonder will my mouth open and say,
'Are you going all the way
to Newcastle?' or 'Can I get you a coffee?'
Or will it simply go 'aaaaah'
as if it had a mind of its own?

Half closing eggshell blue eyes,
she runs her hand through her hair
so that it clings to the carriage cloth,
then slowly frees itself.
She finds a brush and her long fair hair
flies back and forth like an African fly-whisk,
making me feel dizzy.

Suddenly, without warning,
she packs it all away in a rubber band
because I have forgotten to look out
the window for a moment.
A coffee is granted permission
to pass between her lips
and does so eagerly, without fuss.

A tunnel finds us looking out the window
into one another's eyes. She leaves her seat,
but I know that she likes me
because the light saying 'TOILET'
has come on, a sign that she is lifting
her skirt, taking down her pants
and peeing all over my face.

Creative Writing

Trying to persuade about fifteen
Creative Writing students (Poetry)
to put more images into their work,
I was fiddling in my pocket
with an old contraceptive packet,
put there at the start of the course
and long since forgotten about.

If you don't mind my saying so
you seem to see everything
from the man's point of view
exactly like my husband.
What happened to women's poetry
in the last two thousand years?
What about Sappho?
What about Sharon Olds?

The foil wrapper of the Durex Gossamer,
weakened by hours of friction,
gave way and my fingers found themselves
rubbing together in a mess
of spermicide and vaginal lubricant.

Desire

Arching perfectly-plucked eyebrows
over blue eggshell eyes
she tells me it is possible in her country
to go all the way
from Viipuri on the Gulf of Finland
to Jisalmi, far inland,
on little steamers
which thread through channels in the rocks
and forested islands.
Moving her hand through the air
she describes how certain rivers and lakes
cascade into other lakes
in magnificent waterfalls
which provide all the electricity for Finland.

Bath night

A nurse kneels on the floor of the bath house
pulling loose Jim's protective underclothes.
'Washing you,' she murmurs,
touching the marks left by the laces.
'Remember now. Washing you.'

Jim stands up very straight and tall,
his eyes screwed shut.
His toes grip the edge of the bath mat.
'Washing you,' he repeats after her.
'Remember washing you.'

The nurse picks up Jim in her arms
and lets him slip out of the towel
into the disinfected water. His wasted legs
loom to the surface like slender birch trunks.
His feet stand up like pale stalks.

He wheels at anchor now, in his element,
and sometimes he floats free of the dry world
in that narrow white boat
that is going nowhere, wreathed in steam.
And sometimes he remembers her.

'Washing you,' he murmurs, as the green water
laps his body. 'Remember washing you.'
His eyes are screwed shut.
His arms are folded across his chest
as if he is flying into himself.

Post-War British

Everyone screwing up their eyes
as if they can't quite make us out –
Jim with his hair fully restored,
Johnny with the Simoniz duster,
polishing the Jowett Javelin to extinction
as long ago as 1951.

There's no such person as Anne,
but Gar is still there, looking quite like
her old self again, and Mr Burns,
none the worse for New Zealand,
waiting for us to make up our minds:
are we coming with them or not?

The afternoon goes on like that
until we are piling into the car,
trying not to sit in the middle.
Isn't that the anti-carsick chain
hanging down behind, that was supposed to
earth the static electricity?

It doesn't even touch the ground!
The children leaning out of the windows
must be waving goodbye
to their own grandchildren,
but they think they can smell the sea
just over the next horizon.

And here we all are at last –
our faces coming up tired but satisfied
at the other end of our lives,
our knitted bathing-trunks falling down.
The cross-hatched anti-invasion groynes
postmark the scene for us in 1950

and all the dogs that existed then,
named after Sid Field characters,
leaping to within an inch of the stick
that hovers in the air above the sea,
bring it back to us now
and lay it at our feet.

Last goodbyes

On the last day of the holidays
we are dying men,
remembering our lost youth
in the rhododendron trees.
We say goodbye to the hen-house,
the potting shed, the flat roof,
the island with a drawbridge.
We have our last go on the swing
with the table underneath
for launching ourselves off into space.
We swing in a great circle,
pushing ourselves away from the tree
with our feet, till we spin
giddily back to the table again –
all afternoon, till it is time to go.
On the last day of the holidays
we stand completely still,
waiting for the taxi to come,
remembering our lost youth
in the rhododendron trees.

Early morning swim

Every year now you make your face
a little fainter in its vellum photo-frame,
as if you were washing off your make-up with a towel
and catching the last train home.

You have forgotten how to storm
and shout about the place, but not how to gaze
abstractedly over our shoulders into this room
that is not your room any more.

What do you see that we don't see? Why don't you mind
if we are late coming down to breakfast,
or we don't ring up as much as we should?
At this distance, your voice grows fainter on the line,

your words harder to catch. With one hand
you shield your eyes from the sun, as if you have decided
to overlook the way we dress to come up to London
or go to the theatre. You can't see me,

but I can see you, walking away from us, throwing back
your shoulders as you breathe the sea air,
pretending not to limp over the rocky ground.
It is early morning, time for our early morning swim.

You lead the way in your towelling dressing-gown
down the alley behind the hotel, us two boys
sleepwalking along behind you, stumbling
and grumbling a little because it is so early.

We don't understand that this could be our last
swim together, our last chance to prove that we are men.
We don't want to go of course, but we do really.
The water will be cold at this time of day.

Dinner with my mother

My mother is saying 'Now'.
'Now,' she says, taking down a saucepan,
putting it on the stove.
She doesn't say anything else for a while,

so that time passes slowly, on the simmer,
until it is 'Now' again
as she hammers out our steaks
for Steak Diane.

I have to be on hand at times like this
for table-laying,
drink replenishment
and general conversational encouragement,

but I am getting hungry
and there is nowhere to sit down.
'Now,' I say, making a point
of opening a bottle of wine.

My mother isn't listening.
She's miles away,
testing the sauce with a spoon,
narrowing her eyes through the steam.

'Now,' she says very slowly, meaning
which is it to be,
the rosemary or tarragon vinegar
for the salad dressing?

I hold my breath, lest anything
should go wrong at the last minute.
But now it is really 'Now',
our time to sit and eat.

Algarve, 1991

Message not left on an Answerphone
(for C. W.)

As night comes on, I remember we used to play
at this time of day, and you would tell me:
'Don't get excited now, or we'll miss the film.'
You would be sitting on my lap, making a fuss of me.
A shoulder strap would fall down.
A buckle would come away in my hand.
That famous buckle! Did you get it mended yet?
Sometimes the telephone would ring
while we were playing, making us cross,
even though it was still quite early.
You would pick up the phone and talk noncommittally
for a moment or two, because you had to.
How I loved you when you talked like that.
At other times we let the answerphone do the work
and listened to the names of your friends
coming through from another world.
Darling, we made ourselves late sometimes,
playing those games. We made ourselves cry.
Now it is me who hangs endlessly on the line,
who hears your voice repeating at all hours:
'I can't get to the phone at the moment,
but do leave a message.' Pick up the phone, damn you.
Can't you recognize one of my silences by now?

In the blindfold hours

In the blindfold hours,
in the memory wars,
don't fool yourself it never happened,
that you never loved her.
Don't degrade yourself with empty hopes like these.

Go to the window. Listen to the trees.
It is only air we live in.
There is nothing to be frightened of.

Keats

How can I find love in the middle of the night
when the only females out so late
are rag mountains scavenging the bins
behind Indian restaurants? Imagine a dog kennel
made out of old audio cartons. Inside sits a thing
lagged in pink polystyrene, tickling her palm,
blowing out her cheeks at me. She shows me
her business card, an empty sardine tin
attached to a chain round her neck.

I spring forth eagerly, excited by the smell
of sardine oil clinging to her fur. I want to do it
immediately on the pile of old yoghurt pots
and take-away boxes, but she makes me wait

while she slips into something different to go out –
a sheath made of 'I'm Backing Britain' shopping bags,
a veil made of tarred and knotted string.
Like a gigantic hen, she leads the way down Oxford St,
tapping on plate-glass windows with a twig.

Waiting to go on

When I hear the five-minute call
for Orchestra and Beginners
I take my chair upstairs
and sit in the wings in my underpants,
my trousers over one arm.
I'm not in the first scene,
but I don't trust the Tannoy any more
after what happened the other night.
'If you're not coming on, Mr Williams,
that's all right with me,
but for God's sake don't come on late.'

They let the first Walking Gentleman go
after only one warning
just for lying down between the Acts.
They didn't bother auditioning the part,
they recast the suit
and I happened to have short arms.
It's cold sitting here night after night
with nothing over my knees,
but the suit belongs to the Company
and I don't want to be fined
for having poor creases.

Everyone knows this

Every object, every action,
a light suddenly switched on,
a door left open,
carries a hidden watermark
of joy or joylessness,
hope or hopelessness,
which might reveal itself
in the look on someone's face.

Children crying in the next door house,
young men going to work,
the saxophone solo
in 'I'm Gonna Be a Wheel Some Day',
are sorrowful or reassuring
depending on a smell of garlic
drifting up from downstairs,
or the sound of a horse race.

We live in a tiny place
where everything is attached
to something else, more precious.
Dog-barks, head-shakes,
unexpected knocks
bring tears to our eyes.
A box of Brillo pads
comes close to happiness.

Acknowledgements

The poems in this selection are taken from the following books, to whose publishers acknowledgement is made: *Shibboleth* (Oxford University Press, 1988) and *Errata* (Oxford University Press, 1993) for Michael Donaghy; *Dangerous play: Poems 1974– 1984* (Penguin, 1985), *Natural causes* (Chatto, 1987), *Love in a life* (Faber, 1991) and *The price of everything* (Faber, 1994) for Andrew Motion; *Selected poems* (Oxford University Press, 1989), *Self- Portrait with a slide* (Oxford University Press, 1990), and *Dock leaves* (Faber, 1994) for Hugo Williams.

READ MORE IN PENGUIN

In every corner of the world, on every subject under the sun, Penguin represents quality and variety – the very best in publishing today.

For complete information about books available from Penguin – including Puffins, Penguin Classics and Arkana – and how to order them, write to us at the appropriate address below. Please note that for copyright reasons the selection of books varies from country to country.

In the United Kingdom: Please write to *Dept. EP, Penguin Books Ltd, Bath Road, Harmondsworth, West Drayton, Middlesex UB7 0DA*

In the United States: Please write to *Consumer Sales, Penguin USA, P.O. Box 999, Dept. 17109, Bergenfield, New Jersey 07621-0120.* VISA and MasterCard holders call 1-800-253-6476 to order Penguin titles

In Canada: Please write to *Penguin Books Canada Ltd, 10 Alcorn Avenue, Suite 300, Toronto, Ontario M4V 3B2*

In Australia: Please write to *Penguin Books Australia Ltd, P.O. Box 257, Ringwood, Victoria 3134*

In New Zealand: Please write to *Penguin Books (NZ) Ltd, Private Bag 102902, North Shore Mail Centre, Auckland 10*

In India: Please write to *Penguin Books India Pvt Ltd, 706 Eros Apartments, 56 Nehru Place, New Delhi 110 019*

In the Netherlands: Please write to *Penguin Books Netherlands bv, Postbus 3507, NL-1001 AH Amsterdam*

In Germany: Please write to *Penguin Books Deutschland GmbH, Metzlerstrasse 26, 60594 Frankfurt am Main*

In Spain: Please write to *Penguin Books S. A., Bravo Murillo 19, 1° B, 28015 Madrid*

In Italy: Please write to *Penguin Italia s.r.l., Via Felice Casati 20, I–20124 Milano*

In France: Please write to *Penguin France S. A., 17 rue Lejeune, F–31000 Toulouse*

In Japan: Please write to *Penguin Books Japan, Ishikiribashi Building, 2–5–4, Suido, Bunkyo-ku, Tokyo 112*

In South Africa: Please write to *Longman Penguin Southern Africa (Pty) Ltd, Private Bag X08, Bertsham 2013*

READ MORE IN PENGUIN

A SELECTION OF POETRY

American Verse
British Poetry since 1945
Caribbean Verse in English
Chinese Love Poetry
A Choice of Comic and Curious Verse
Contemporary American Poetry
Contemporary British Poetry
Contemporary Irish Poetry
English Poetry 1918–60
English Romantic Verse
English Verse
First World War Poetry
German Verse
Greek Verse
Homosexual Verse
Imagist Poetry
Irish Verse
Japanese Verse
The Metaphysical Poets
Modern African Poetry
New Poetry
Poetry of the Thirties
Scottish Verse
Surrealist Poetry in English
Spanish Verse
Victorian Verse
Women Poets
Zen Poetry

POETRY LIBRARY

Blake	Selected by W. H. Stevenson
Browning	Selected by Daniel Karlin
Burns	Selected by Angus Calder and William Donnelly
Byron	Selected by A. S. B. Glover
Clare	Selected by Geoffrey Summerfield
Coleridge	Selected by Richard Holmes
Donne	Selected by John Hayward
Dryden	Selected by Douglas Grant
Hardy	Selected by David Wright
Housman	Introduced by John Sparrow
Keats	Selected by John Barnard
Kipling	Selected by Craig Raine
Lawrence	Selected by Keith Sagar
Milton	Selected by Laurence D. Lerner
Pope	Selected by Douglas Grant
Rubáiyát of Omar Khayyám	Translated by Edward FitzGerald
Shelley	Selected by Isabel Quigly
Tennyson	Selected by W. E. Williams
Wordsworth	Selected by Nicholas Roe
Yeats	Selected by Timothy Webb

READ MORE IN PENGUIN

A SELECTION OF POETRY

James Fenton   Out of Danger

A collection wonderfully open to experience – of foreign places, differences, feelings and languages.

U. A. Fanthorpe   Selected Poems

'She is an erudite poet, rich in experience and haunted by the classical past ... fully at home in the world of the turbulent NHS, the decaying academies, and all the draughty corners of the abandoned Welfare State' – *Observer*

Craig Raine   Clay. Whereabouts Unknown

'I cannot think of anyone else writing today whose every line is so unfailingly exciting' – *Sunday Times*

Marge Piercy   Eight Chambers of the Heart

Marge Piercy's poetry is written to be read and spoken aloud, to move, provoke and entertain, on every subject under the sun from ecology to cats and cookery, to political, sexual and family relationships.

Joseph Brodsky   To Urania
Winner of the 1987 Nobel Prize for Literature

Exiled from the Soviet Union in 1972, Joseph Brodsky has been universally acclaimed as the most talented Russian poet of his generation.

Paul Celan   Selected Poems
Winner of the first European Translation Prize, 1990

'The English reader can now enter the hermetic universe of a German–Jewish poet who made out of the anguish of his people, things of terror and beauty' – *The Times Literary Supplement*

Geoffrey Hill   Canaan

'Among our finest poets, Geoffrey Hill is at present the most European – in his Latinity, in his dramatization of the Christian condition, in his political intensity' – *Sunday Times*